THE KIM & KRICKITT
CARPENTER STORY

The Vow

KIM & KRICKITT
CARPENTER

WITH JOHN PERRY

BROADMAN
&HOLMAN
PUBLISHERS

NASHVILLE, TENNESSEE

0–8054–2130–0

Published by Broadman & Holman Publishers,
Nashville, Tennessee

Unless otherwise noted, Scripture quotations are from the New American Standard Bible, © the Lockman Foundation, 1960, 1962, 1963, 1968, 1971, 1972, 1973, 1975, 1977; used by permission. Quotations marked NIV are from the Holy Bible, New International Version, © 1973, 1978, 1984 by International Bible Society.

Dewey Decimal Classification: 616
Subject Heading: BIOGRAPHY

Library of Congress Cataloging-in-Publication Data
Carpenter, Kim, 1965–
    The vow : the Kim and Krickitt Carpenter story / Kim & Krickitt
Carpenter, with John Perry.
        p. cm.
    ISBN 0–8054–2130–0
    1. Carpenter, Krickitt, 1969—Health. 2. Coma—Patients—New
Mexico—Biography. 3. Christian biography—New Mexico. I. Carpenter,
Krickitt, 1969– . II. Perry, John, 1952– . III. Title.

RB150.C6 C37   2000
616.8'49—dc21
[B]
                                                    00–027793

3 4 5 04 03 02 01 00

CONTENTS

PREFACE

*W*hen our story first started getting media attention, someone advised us to enjoy it while we could because in six months it would all be over.

That was just before our second wedding ceremony in 1996, which was already almost three years after the traffic accident that changed our lives so dramatically. Yet here we are, still getting calls from talk-show producers, still speaking to audiences and congregations across the country about our experience, still sharing our story with newfound friends.

As we pieced our lives and our marriage back together, we prayed that God would use our trials for some great purpose. The continued interest in our story has been an answer to that prayer. We've had the chance to share our experience with TV audiences on *Oprah, Inside Edition, Leeza, Day & Date, Signs & Wonders, Crook & Chase, The 700 Club,* and many other shows in the United States, Europe, and Asia. As this book goes to press, we have return visits pending on several of them. Leading magazines including *People, Reader's Digest,* and *McCall's* have written about us. And a major Hollywood studio is currently at work on the screenplay for a feature film.

Out of everything we've done, though, this book is where our heart is. A few minutes on the air or a few pages in a magazine are wonderful ways to reach out to a large audience, but they don't give us a chance to tell the whole story or tell it exactly the way we feel it inside. With a book, we can say everything that's important to us about what has happened in our lives, how these events changed and strengthened us, and where we're headed from here. We also have the freedom to make it clear that without God, there would be no story at all. (We declined an offer to appear on one of the most popular prime-time network talk shows because the producer told us we wouldn't be allowed to bring up anything spiritual. It would have been impossible to share our story truthfully with that limitation.)

While we've put everything we have into this book, the end result is the work of many hands. We thank Len Goss, our editor at Broadman & Holman, and John Perry, who captured our words and ideas on paper. Most of all we thank the people who have shared in the story by encouraging and supporting us along the way:

DJ Coombs and Drs. Beamsley, Kennedy, and Rosendale, who preserved Krickitt's life through those first terrifying hours in Gallup; Bob Grothe and Dennis Keys, who got her to Albuquerque still breathing; Drs. Singh and Klonoff and others at Barrow Neurological Institute in Phoenix, who helped restore her dignity and capabilities;

Wayne and Kelli Marshall, our first prayer warriors; Scott Madsen, "physical terrorist" and a rock of friendship and assurance at the height of the storm; Matt Klonowski, always there when the going got toughest; Rachael Rosen, Kristi Pinnick, Lisa Eberly Seifen, Megan Almquist Jones, Katie Devore Fuhr, Heather Toomey, Julie Vander Dussen de Jong, Lisa Dolan, Dawn Morano, Tracy Saxen,

Arvin and Shirley Blome, Corky and Sally Morris, Mike Kloeppel, Curtis and Wendy Jones, Richard L. Gerding, and other friends who visited Krickitt in the hospital and encouraged her through many months of rehab;

Rob Evers, whose wise counsel and generosity were truly a godsend; Juan Galvan and members of the Highlands Cowboys, for showing the world what real teamwork is all about; Tom Colbert, who guided us in our first halting steps into the media world; Lynn Rogers, the Cal State gymnastics coach who inspired his team to "go for it" in life as well as in gymnastics; Paul Taublieb, Roger Birnbaum, and John Glickman, who have believed in our story enough to shepherd it through the Hollywood moviemaking maze.

This is also the story of a family that has worked, prayed, laughed, cried, and rejoiced together, and one that God is still shaping, refining, and teaching to follow him: Gus and Mary, Danny and Mo, Jamey and Gretchen, Kirk and Teresa, Kelly and Julie. They all brought us the comfort, encouragement, assurance, and love that only family can bring.

Above all the rest, we give glory to God for his goodness. By his grace he saved us from being just another obituary in a New Mexico newspaper, and has given us both the ability and the burden to sing his praises to the world.

It's a song we delight in.

Kim and Krickitt Carpenter
Farmington, New Mexico
Valentine's Day, 2000

Chapter 1

THE JOURNEY BEGINS

*H*ey, Krick, you gonna take all day?" As I hollered toward the open door, she came bounding out of the apartment toward the car, which I was trying to stuff with enough luggage for a Thanksgiving weekend and still leave room for the two of us and a friend we were dropping off at the airport in Phoenix.

"Here I am," she announced, half walking, half skipping across the sidewalk, her blue eyes bright in the afternoon sun, its rays picking up the red highlights in her dark chestnut hair. When I looked at her, she was already looking at me.

"I love you, Kimmer," she said, suddenly soft and still. "I love you, Krickitt," I answered. I kissed her across the stack of shopping bags in her arms. The bags made a loud crumpling sound as we pressed up against them, but the noise didn't seem to bother Krickitt. I know it didn't bother me.

It would be our first Thanksgiving as Mr. and Mrs. Kim J. Carpenter, and I had more to be thankful for than I could ever imagine. I had a dream job coaching college baseball at New Mexico Highlands University. I was also associate athletic director there, with practically unlimited opportunity for the future. But most of all I was married to Krisxan Pappas Carpenter, a witty, fun-loving, effervescent young woman with the figure of a college gymnast (which she was) and the rock-solid faith of someone who believes unconditionally in the sovereignty, power, and saving grace of Jesus Christ (which she did).

While Krickitt wedged the shopping bags into the trunk, I went back for one last look to see if we'd left anything, then locked the door behind me. New Mexico nights are brisk in November and the temperature was already starting to drop. Though it had been comfortable during the day, it would be just a few degrees above freezing by midnight. By then we'd be snuggled under the covers at Krickitt's parents' house in Phoenix, looking forward to building a holiday tradition together.

As the breeze picked up, it was hard to believe that less than two months ago we'd been on our honeymoon in Hawaii—warm sand, endless summer, tropical paradise. Now it was already Thanksgiving. Santa had been at the mall for two weeks, and the stores were jammed from wall to wall with Christmas displays. Time was moving too fast. We were excited about spending our first Christmas together, first New Year's, first Valentine's Day, first National Kumquat Week, and all the rest. I wanted to savor every day. Besides, I already had the best Christmas gift the world had to offer, and she was sitting in the front seat waiting for me to get in.

"Hey, Kimmer, you gonna take all day?" She tried to be serious, but her thousand-megawatt smile fought its way to the surface. We laughed. We kissed (no shopping bags this time). I started the car, backed out of the parking lot, and eased into the holiday traffic.

We had a long trip ahead of us, but an easy one, from our home in Las Vegas, New Mexico, through Santa Fe, Albuquerque, and Flagstaff, with interstate all the way. A friend from school was hitching a ride with us to catch a plane in Phoenix. Originally we had planned to leave in the morning in order to get to the Pappas house before dark, but our passenger had a test after lunch. By the time we picked him up and headed southwest on I–25, it was already after two o'clock. It would be close to midnight by the time we pulled in.

With all I had to look forward to and be thankful for already, there was still one more thing I was really excited about that morning: peanut butter and jelly. I am a pushover for a good PB&J, and until I got married, had considered them essential to life as we know it. But with her years of gymnastics training and conditioning as backup, Krickitt pronounced this great American delicacy to be junk food (!) and proceeded to give me more or less constant grief about my craving for it. This weekend, however, in an awesome show of reconciliation and selflessness, she had not only allowed them in her presence, she actually made some to eat in the car! Every so often I would imagine how delicious they were going to taste later on. Occasionally I got a whiff of peanut butter from the box where the car munchies were packed. It was going to be incredible.

We sailed through Santa Fe and Albuquerque, but soon after we turned west on I–40 toward the Arizona border, I started feeling a cold coming on. I thought I could shake it off, but Krickitt noticed something wasn't right.

"Kimmer, you don't look so good. Are you all right?"

"I've got a little bug or something. Be OK in a few minutes."

But I wasn't OK in a few minutes, I was worse. By the time Krickitt said we ought to stop for some medicine, I was in no shape to argue with her. We pulled off the highway and into a convenience store. Krickitt and I went in and picked out something to ease my symptoms, along with a soft drink to take the capsules with.

"Maybe I should drive a little while," she said, her voice tinged with concern. "I don't mind. Then you can lay down in the backseat and get some rest."

I felt truly awful. It was an offer I was glad to accept.

"Thanks, lovey. This isn't how I planned to impress the in-laws on our first holiday with them."

She smiled that smile again. I smiled back as well as I could, which was pretty lame by comparison but it was the best I could do considering. Krickitt took the wheel while I tried to stretch out in back. Our Ford Escort was brand new but not designed with sleeping baseball coaches in mind. It was a tight squeeze. However, its saving grace was that it was a hatchback, and with the back of the rear seat folded down I could stretch my legs out into the trunk. I laid down behind Krickitt and tried to get comfortable while I waited for the cold capsules to kick in. Krickitt got back on the interstate, following the setting sun west toward Phoenix and our journey's end. As bad as I felt, I still had the energy to reach around the front seat headrest and flick Krickitt's ear once in awhile, just to make sure she didn't forget about me.

A little after six in the afternoon we passed through Gallup, the last big town before the New Mexico/Arizona border. Dusk doesn't last long in the thin desert atmosphere, and after sunset the darkness comes fast. Krickitt turned the headlights on, adding the soft glow of the instrument panel to the harsh glare of oncoming lights that played across her face. It was still too light for me to pick out any constellations through the back window, but the sky glowed purple at the horizon, and the evening star shone all alone like a diamond on velvet.

Sitting up and lying down and sitting up again, trying to get comfortable, I finally dozed off with my head at the back of the driver's seat and my legs extending straight behind me into the trunk. Suddenly I was jolted awake as the car decelerated rapidly and swerved to the left. I raised up just in time to see the image of headlights behind us zooming leftward in the driver's side mirror, very large at first, then completely filling the mirror in a split second.

"Watch out!" our passenger shouted.

Krickitt's only response was a horrifying scream.

I don't remember hearing anything after that, or feeling any pain, but I recall every sensation of movement that took place over the next several seconds. My face was suddenly jammed between the side of Krickitt's seat and her door. My head was jerked back. Then I rolled over to the other side of the car and hit the wheelwell with my rib cage. There was a momentary floating sensation, a slow-motion twisting and tumbling like the dream sequence in a movie. I saw sparks and thought the car was on fire. I felt a strange tingling sensation in my back. Then everything was still.

I didn't know exactly what happened in those few seconds until much later when I read the highway patrolman's report. It said that at approximately 6:30 p.m. on November 24, 1993, 5.7 miles east of the Arizona/New Mexico state line, a white Ford Escort was involved in a collision with two trucks.

Later investigations fleshed out the story. That November evening a red flatbed truck traveling west on I–40 with a load of car parts started having engine trouble. The driver slowed to about 25 miles per hour in the right lane. Traveling at highway speed, Krickitt came up behind the truck, which was hidden in a cloud of black smoke produced by a defective fuel filter.

Though the flatbed's emergency flashers weren't on, Krickitt saw slow-moving taillights loom into view through the exhaust cloud, braked hard, and swerved to the left. At the same moment a pickup truck following close behind our car swerved left too.

The right front fender of the Escort clipped the left rear corner of the flatbed. Then as the car started to swerve and Krickitt struggled for control, the pickup came up from behind and rammed us broadside. The impact sent our car careening into the air. It sailed 30 feet, slammed back to the ground, rolled onto its roof, back around upright, onto the roof again, then slid upside down for 106 feet and stopped on the shoulder of the road.

In that first instant of stillness I was too stunned to say anything. When I could think again, I didn't think about the chance that I might be hurt. I couldn't feel a thing. All I could think of was Krickitt.

"Krickitt!" I screamed. No answer. "Krickiiiiitt!!" I recognized the sound of the car engine running, so I knew I could hear, but there was no answer. I looked around. After a second I realized the car was on its top and I was lying inside on the roof. The sunroof had been shattered during the long, final skid, and the last part of that 106-foot trip had been made on broken glass and bare skin.

I screamed for Krickitt again, and as the sound of my voice died away, I had a sensation of my face being wet. As much as we'd been tossed around, I was probably cut and bleeding. I tried to raise my hand up to my face to feel if I was injured. Slowly my hand came forward, dreamlike, as if it were somebody else's hand. As it got closer to me a red splotch appeared on it, then another. The hand itself didn't seem to be hurt, but I knew that scalp wounds bled like crazy and I was probably bleeding on myself.

I tried to stop the splotches by holding the hand away from my face. Still they kept coming. The red ran down my arm and started dripping onto the broken sunroof. Then I looked up. In this upside-down world, I was where the floor should have been. It was strange to look up where the roof should have been and see the floor there with the seats fastened to it, headrests pointing down at me.

The dripping blood wasn't mine. Overhead, suspended in mid-air by her seat belt, my wife was dying. Her arms dangled limp. Her eyes were closed. She didn't move. We weren't more than a couple of feet apart but I couldn't reach her. It was almost dark and I couldn't see her clearly enough to tell what was wrong, or whether she was actually dead already.

"Krickitt!" I snapped in as much of my hard-nosed coach/drill sergeant voice as I could muster, hoping to penetrate her consciousness. Her eyes didn't open, but she stirred a little. Then she let out a long, ragged, sighing breath and was still again.

I thought it was the last breath she would ever take.

I called her name again and started trying to get out of the car, but I couldn't move. There wasn't anything on top of me or in my way, and I had a clear shot out of the car through the back side window since the glass was completely gone. But there was no feeling in my legs. I was paralyzed from the waist down.

My nose had a strange tingly sensation. I reached up to touch it and felt something sharp. It was the bone at the base of where my nose should have been. Lower on my face I felt what I first thought was a badly swollen lip. It was my nose, hanging down in front of my mouth by a flap of skin.

I saw a face through the window. "Give me your hand! I'll help you out!" the stranger shouted.

"I can't move my legs," I shouted back.

"This thing's liable to explode. Turn the motor off!" Our passenger, who had been riding shotgun, was miraculously spared with only a separated shoulder. He had already gotten out of the car and reached back in to get to the ignition.

"The key's broken off," he said.

"You've got to get it turned off!" the stranger answered. After some desperate jiggling and twisting, the ignition switch turned and the engine fell silent.

The man was a trucker who had stopped to see if he could help. "I'm coming to get you," he said. Dropping to his stomach, he low crawled into the car on his knees and elbows through the window beside me. I grabbed him around the shoulders. He held on to me with one hand, and used the other to help scoot us backward out of the car and over to the grass beside the highway.

I saw then that somebody else had stopped. A husband and wife parked and came over, leaving three or four children in their van. "You kids stay inside and pray," the man instructed as he walked toward our car. He looked around at all the wreckage and blood and, without any show of panic or defeat, put his hand on one of the upturned tires and started praying. His wife came over to me in the grass and thought I was bleeding to death. That was before she knew a lot of the blood on me wasn't mine.

The couple introduced themselves as Wayne and Kelli Marshall and offered to do whatever they could to help. At the moment, I wasn't sure what to ask for other than for Krickitt to wake up.

As the trucker wrapped me in blankets from his cab, another motorist stopped and hurried over to me. She said a few words, then stopped abruptly with a shock of horrified recognition on her face. "Good Lord! You're Danny Carpenter's son! Your cousin Debbie and I are best friends!"

Here we were in the middle of nowhere and had already encountered three people whose presence could only be blessings from an all-sovereign Lord: a rescuer, a prayer warrior, and a family friend.

"I'll get hold of your family," she said, and left the scene a few minutes later to start making calls.

Drivers of the other two vehicles had no visible injuries, and the two passengers in the pickup had relatively minor wounds. That left Krickitt and me. I was numb with shock. All I could think about was her trapped inside that twisted lump of steel a few feet away, looking like she was bleeding to death if she weren't already dead. Her head was caught between the steering wheel and the roof where the top had been crushed during the rollover. (If I'd been driving I would have been killed instantly, because I wouldn't have fit in the space remaining after the impact and my skull would have been crushed.) Unlatching her seat belt before her head was free would probably break her neck. If it wasn't already broken.

Within minutes the police and ambulances started arriving. Krickitt would have to be cut out of the car, but the EMTs were afraid to wait that long to start treatment. So one of them, DJ Coombs, crawled inside the car—not even mentioning that she had severe claustrophobia—and started giving Krickitt IVs and monitoring her vital signs there, still hanging upside down from the seat belt. Krick seemed to drift in and out of consciousness, her pupils alternately constricted and dilated—a classic symptom, I later learned, of severe brain injury.

Our passenger and I were loaded into an ambulance while the rescue team was still cutting open the car. On the way to the hospital in Gallup, the EMTs began cataloguing my injuries. My left ear was almost torn off, my nose nearly severed. I also had other facial lacerations, a concussion, two cracked ribs, and a broken hand. Later, doctors would add a punctured lung and bruised heart muscle to the list.

I heard the ambulance attendant call the hospital on the radio. "We have two male accident victims, one in critical condition, one serious. The third victim is still at the scene in severely critical condition." That meant at least she was still alive.

We pulled into the emergency entrance of Rehoboth-McKinley Christian Hospital in Gallup. I went for an X-ray of a big knot behind my left ear that they thought might indicate a skull fracture. When I got finished, Krick was already in intensive care so I didn't see her when I came in, but I could tell the news wasn't good. It had taken more than half an hour to cut her out of the car. Nobody would give me a straight answer about her condition. How was she? Was she going to recover? Was she going to be OK? I didn't know until later that when one of the ambulance technicians heard Krickitt was still alive hours after being admitted to the hospital, she refused to believe it. She'd never seen anyone survive such massive head trauma.

As soon as Krickitt arrived, she got all the attention, which was fine with me. The ER team had given me some preliminary treatment, but I didn't want to take any sedative or have any other work done until I knew what was happening with my wife. I'd been waiting in the ER for awhile when a doctor who'd been working on

Krickitt in the trauma room came over to me. His manner was professional and confident, even though his eyes were tired. He handed me a little manila envelope.

"Mr. Carpenter, I'm terribly sorry."

Before I could think of anything to say, the doctor left the room. I opened the envelope with my good hand and slid the contents out into the broken one. There was Krickitt's Highlands University watch I'd had made for her. And her wedding ring.

Till death do us part.

My thoughts were all scrambled up inside me. I was in pain now, and exhausted, and annoyed that I didn't know where Krickitt was or what was going on with her. But at that instant, piercing through everything else like a rifle shot, was the thought that she was dead.

I was too incredulous to be sad. Not that I wasn't willing to believe it, though I didn't want to. I couldn't believe it. Was incapable of believing it. I could not accept the fact that I had caressed that beautiful face for the last time. That those shining eyes were closed forever. That I would never again see those thousand megawatts blazing at me across the dinner table. I couldn't believe that the most joyful, most enthusiastic Christian I had ever known could be torn from my life so savagely. That after ten weeks of marriage I was a widower.

I don't know how long it was before a nurse came in. "We've done all we can, and she hasn't improved," she said. "She's beyond medical help." *Beyond medical help, maybe,* I thought. *But not beyond God's.*

The nurse continued. "Still, she's hanging in there better than anybody thought she would. She's strong, and she's in excellent physical condition. The doctor has called Lifeguard One to see if they can airlift her to Albuquerque."

The door that had seemed shut and sealed only minutes ago had miraculously opened a crack. *I can do all things through Christ who strengthens me.*

I didn't know it then, but when the medical flight team got orders to fly Krick 130 miles to the University of New Mexico Medical Center in Albuquerque, they were afraid, based on their experience, that it would be a wasted trip. It would take a solid hour for them to get to Gallup, and the same to get to UNMC. By then it could easily be too late.

As they wheeled her out of intensive care to get ready for the flight, I saw Krickitt for the first time since the ambulance had pulled away from the accident hours before. She was lying on a gurney, surrounded by nurses and orderlies overseeing what looked like about a dozen IV lines and monitors. Her head and face were so swollen and bruised that I could hardly recognize her. Her lips and ears were blue-black, and the swelling was so bad that her eyelids couldn't close all the way. Her eyes, when they were open, looked to the right with a blank stare, and her arms moved around aimlessly (more signs, I later learned, of severe head injury). Her body temperature was unstable, so they had put her in a big thermal wrap. It looked like a body bag.

I got up off of my bed and grabbed both of her hands. They were shockingly cold. "We're gonna get through this, Krick," I said to her. "We're gonna make it." I smiled but felt the tears coming just the same. "Don't you die on me!" I said, my mouth inches from her face. She was wearing an oxygen mask and I could hear her breathing, shallow and tentative. "We're lifetime buddies, remember? We've got a long way to go!"

It wasn't until they began wheeling her out to the helipad that I realized they had no intention of taking me with them.

"They have to have two medics and a lot of gear to give your wife any chance for survival," somebody was saying. "There's no room for a passenger."

I wasn't a passenger; I was her husband. I was also a patient, by the way, with broken bones and still-undiagnosed respiratory problems. I wanted them to come back for me.

"There are two other active calls," somebody answered. "There's no way we can make another two-hour round trip to Albuquerque with you." The cluster of people with Krickitt in the middle went through a set of swinging doors.

"Hang in there, babe, I'm praying for you!" I sobbed through the window at the silent form on the gurney. I watched the nurses roll her up to the waiting helicopter and ease her inside, then listened as the flump-flump-flump of its overhead rotor faded into the distance.

Ever since I'd arrived at the hospital, I'd tried repeatedly to get in touch with Krickitt's parents in Phoenix and mine in Farmington. The day before Thanksgiving, nobody was home. Running out of options, I finally called Krickitt's old number and talked to her ex-roommate Lisa Eberly, who still lived with Megan Almquist in the apartment the three of them once shared. I gave her a quick rundown of the situation, then asked her to try and reach Krickitt's folks, tell them we'd been in a wreck, and stand by for further news.

Next I called my boss at the university, athletic director Rob Evers. I told him we'd been in a wreck and didn't know if Krickitt would make it. I couldn't find my parents and needed him to track them down. He said he'd take care of it and immediately started on the trail. He knew I had an uncle in Albuquerque, last name Morris, but didn't know his first name because everyone called him "Corky." He told the telephone operator he had an emergency and had to contact the family. "We don't usually do this," the operator explained, "but stay on the line." She called every Morris in Albuquerque until she found the right one—James C.

Uncle Corky gave him Dad's business partner's phone number. His partner knew Dad was in Roswell to spend Thanksgiving with my brother Kelly and got him on his cell phone. Dad called the hospital immediately, and I explained the situation. Krickitt was in bad shape. They'd already given me her wedding ring in a manila envelope.

I called him again after Krickitt's chopper took off. I'm sure he answered on the first ring, but by the time I started talking I was crying so hard he could hardly understand me.

"They've flown Krickitt to Albuquerque and they wouldn't let me go with her. You've got to come and get me. Take me to her." I could feel the sobs welling up in waves. The lost, abject sobs of a broken child.

"God willing, I've got to see her again before she dies."

Chapter 2

TILL DEATH DO US PART

*K*rickitt's parents, Gus and Mary Pappas, had gone all out to make our first holiday as a married couple something really special. Since Krick and I wouldn't be able to make it to their house for Christmas on account of my schedule at Highlands, they'd already strung their Christmas lights inside and out to give us an advance taste of Yuletide cheer. Earlier in the day, Mary had made rolls and pumpkin pie to take to the big Thanksgiving dinner we were all planning to share with Krickitt's sister-in-law's family in Phoenix. Gus and Mary weren't expecting us to get in from Las Vegas until late, so they'd gone out to a University of Arizona basketball game in Tucson, leaving the inside Christmas lights on to welcome us.

Krickitt's mom knew something was wrong even before they walked in the door. It was after midnight, and when they pulled in there was no white Escort in the driveway. Soon they heard the news that is a parent's worst nightmare: their only daughter had been in a car wreck and would probably be dead by the time they got to her.

Meanwhile I was trying to tell my dad what happened. By now we were both crying, and he could hardly understand me because my broken ribs made it so hard and so painful for me to breathe. I gave him the number I was calling from, and he said he'd put a plan together and call right back.

While I was waiting I got a call from Mary saying Krickitt's friend Lisa Eberly had finally reached them. Krickitt was on her way to Albuquerque, so I couldn't give her any sort of update. She said she would call the University of New Mexico Medical Center to see what was happening, and they'd catch the first plane they could. It would be 8 a.m. the next morning, Thanksgiving Day, before they could fly out.

I don't know if it was two minutes or two hours after Mary and I hung up that I picked up the phone again and heard my dad's voice.

"Son, how are you?"

"I want to see Krickitt, that's how I am. I can't breathe and my back is killing me. I've got to see her, Dad." I felt the tears coming again, but I had to hold on.

"Listen, Son." He was steady as a rock now. It felt so good to think somebody was finally in control who could get me back to Krickitt. "I'll drop your mother off at the hospital in Albuquerque. Then I'll meet you at the truck stop in Grants and drive you back to see Krickitt."

He made it sound like a little jaunt across town. He and Mom had just driven almost four hundred miles diagonally across New Mexico from Farmington to Roswell. There, he was two hundred miles from Albuquerque and another sixty or more from Grants, halfway between Albuquerque and Gallup. A storm had blown in during the night, and some sections of the highway were solid sheets of ice.

"But Dad, I don't think I can get out of here unless you come and get me discharged. They admitted me through the ER, and they haven't even done anything to me yet because they were so busy with Krickitt."

"I'll send Porky to get you out."

I was as good as gone.

Porky Abeda was one of Dad's best friends, a big bear of a man and former fire chief of Gallup. Everybody knew him, and he knew everybody. When I told the hospital staff I was leaving, the nurse argued that there was no way I should be released.

"We haven't had a chance to examine you for internal injuries." I think she was sort of surprised that anyone in the shape I was in could even talk, much less tell her I was headed for the door.

"I just want to be with my wife."

"By the time you get to Albuquerque, it may be impossible to repair the damage to your nose and your ear. We don't know what internal bleeding you might have." A pause, and a very stern look. "If you leave the hospital now, you could die."

"I don't care. If Krickitt dies, I don't want to live."

You're supposed to be a relative before the hospital will release a patient to your care against medical advice. Porky doesn't particularly look like my kin—he's full-blooded Navajo—but whatever he said, he got me out of there, wrapped me in a blanket (somewhere along the way the hospital had cut my clothes off, and we didn't waste time looking for them), bundled me into the backseat, and headed for the truck stop in Grants.

I lay curled up in the blanket trying to find a position where I could breathe with less pain. Every time I inhaled it felt like somebody was touching a branding iron to my chest. Looking up through the window, I watched the freeway lights going by for awhile, then saw the huge truck stop sign as we pulled into the parking lot.

I could see Dad pacing on the sidewalk. He had made the drive from Roswell in record time despite the highway being coated with a treacherous, invisible, mirror-slick sheet of frozen precipitation known as "black ice," and in spite of two other wrecks between Albuquerque and Gallup that night—the same wrecks that tied up the emergency air transportation I had wanted to take me to Krickitt. Porky hopped out of the car and I watched Dad trot up to him.

"Where's Kim?" I heard him ask, his question mixed in with the muffled racket of a dozen tractor-trailer rigs idling all around us. He looked at the car, obviously expecting me to bound out behind Porky and get in his car for the run back to Albuquerque.

"Danny," Porky said solemnly, "Kim's in no shape to get out of the car."

The two of them walked quickly to the car and Porky opened the back door. The icy wind bit into my skin through the blanket. As my father's eyes met mine, he glanced at my cut-up face, ripped ear, and mutilated nose, shivered involuntarily and whispered, "Oh Jesus, God."

The two of them got me into Dad's car, and we took off for what is usually an hour's drive between Grants and Albuquerque. This would be a quicker trip. By the time he got to the on-ramp, Dad was doing a hundred and ten.

I lay on the seat, still trying to find a comfortable position. Nothing seemed to help. I was gurgling more with every breath, unable to get enough air, and the branding iron felt like it had big weights on it now, so that inhaling deeply had gone from painful to impossible.

Dad and I didn't talk much. Every once in awhile he'd say, "Are you all right, Son?"

I thought that no, I wasn't all right. My wife was dying, and I might be dying too. We had been married ten weeks, and now it was all going to be over in a matter of hours if it wasn't over already. But all I could say was, "Just get me to Albuquerque."

Dad called Mom at the hospital every few minutes on the cellular phone. After every call I asked him if there was any news. "They're still working on her," was all he'd say. I didn't know until later that he had called the hospital hours earlier when he was still in Roswell, and was told that she probably wouldn't make it through the night.

We sailed along the interstate at two miles a minute now, in and out of freezing rain. There were times I thought I would never take another breath. The broken ribs had perforated my lungs, and they were slowly filling with blood, suffocating me by inches.

I knew Dad wasn't telling me everything he knew about Krickitt. I had seen her on the way to the helipad in Gallup. I'd heard the ER doctors and nurses talking. They had brought me her wedding ring and said, "Mr. Carpenter, I'm terribly sorry." It seemed to me they had written her off before they even sent her to the hospital in Albuquerque.

I felt in my heart Krickitt was dead. I had told the hospital staff in Gallup that if she died I didn't want to live, and I absolutely meant it. There was an easy way to end this agony. Simply reach up, give the door handle a yank, and roll out. At a hundred and twenty miles an hour it was a sure thing.

But in that moment I felt a strong, serene presence in the car with me that could only have been the Spirit of God. The presence said, "Wait a minute." I couldn't say if they were words I heard or words I felt, but they were there, and they saved me from the most horribly selfish and sinful decision I ever could have made. I don't know if I ever actually reached for the door handle or not, but I know I never considered it again.

Finally we came over a rise and saw the city of Albuquerque spread out on the desert floor below. Propped up on the seat now, I looked down at the galaxy of lights shimmering in the distance and wondered which one of them was closest to the face of the woman I loved so deeply and completely. Which one was guiding the doctors' hands as they struggled to save her life?

Five blocks from the University of New Mexico Medical Center, Dad called the hospital emergency room and told them to be ready for us. It was 4 A.M., ten hours after the accident, and I still hadn't had anything but basic first aid. By the time we rounded the last corner and pulled up to the emergency entrance, there was a crowd waiting—two doctors, three nurses, and Mom. I took that as another bad sign.

The door opened and I tried to get out of the car. I saw Mom look at me, and watched as her expression turned from concerned to shocked and horrified at the sight of my disfigured face. Then she disappeared, crowded out by orderlies and doctors huddling around to help me out of the car, talking to me and to one another so fast it all ran together.

"Where's Krickitt? Where's my wife?" I shouted above the noise as loud as I could. Nobody seemed to be listening. "Somebody please tell me what's happened to my wife!"

Suddenly out of the din I heard a familiar voice booming at me. "Coming through! Coming through! Look out!" It was Mike Kloeppel, another bear of a man who was coming along in the nick of time just like Porky Abeda had done. Mike had been best man at our wedding. He knew what I wanted to know and was barreling through the mob to tell me about Krickitt, pulling nurses and other ER staff away as he came. Somebody grabbed him by the shirt and he shrugged them off, elbows flying like an NBA rebounder.

As soon as he got close enough to be sure I could hear him, he hollered, "She's still hanging in there, Kim. They're still working on her in the ICU."

Our God is an awesome God.

The ER welcoming committee swept me into the emergency room. Getting a good look at my injuries for the first time, the doctors couldn't believe I had been released from the hospital in Gallup in the shape I was in. (What they didn't know is that I released myself against medical advice.)

Physicians who had been working on Krickitt came to check me out and started shouting for IVs, X-rays, and CAT scans, and nurses went flying in every direction. Because of the knot behind my injured ear, they thought I might have brain swelling and permanent damage of my own.

A doctor asked me where I hurt. "My back," I said. "I can hardly move without pains shooting all the way up and down it." They rolled me over to check it out. I heard somebody say, "My God, look at that!" During the wreck, I had been lying against the inside surface of the sunroof as the car slid upside down for more than a hundred feet. The highway pavement had shattered the sunroof glass and driven the slivers into my back. Some of them were four inches long.

The doctor pulled a curtain around me, but I could still hear him exploding. "What the Sam Hill did those people in Gallup think they were doing? Why in the world would they release a patient like this?! Get a team on this man." Of course, he didn't know the whole story.

Krickitt had needed the hospital's undivided attention, and I was glad to have them give it to her. (The Lifeguard One flight nurses would later confirm the quality of care Krickitt received in Gallup, writing, "The major credit for your recovery goes to the Gallup EMTs at the scene and Drs. Kennedy and Beamsley at Rehoboth Hospital. They did all the right things. We just flew as fast as we could.") Besides, I had left the hospital in Gallup over the strongest possible protest from the medical staff there.

As the doctors worked, I kept asking Mom about Krickitt. More than anything in the world I wanted her to tell me Krick was going to be all right. She wouldn't say it. What she knew and I didn't was that none of the helicopter team expected her to survive. The admitting physician in Albuquerque had given her less than a 1 percent chance. She was way into miracle territory.

My twin brother, Kirk, arrived from Farmington, our hometown in northwestern New Mexico near the Four Corners. He and his wife had returned home late from a party and hadn't gotten the news until after midnight.

"How you doin', Kimbo?" he asked, doing his best to smile.

"Been better," I answered. "I gotta see Krickitt."

"You will," he said. "Just hold on until they're ready for you."

Kirk's wife, Teresa, had the most honest reaction of anybody there that night. She took one look at me, covered her face, and ran out of the room. At one time or another I'm sure we all wished we could have done the same thing.

Through all this the ER team was fantastic. They got my face put back together, set my broken hand, worked on my ribs, gave me a sedative, and got ready to admit me. I told them I still wanted to see my wife as soon as possible.

"After you're admitted, you won't be able to go see your wife," someone explained.

"Then you're not admitting me."

They argued, I didn't. No Krickitt, no admission.

Finally they agreed to send me to the recovery room and then let me see Krickitt. She was still in the ICU, and they said they'd take me there in a wheelchair. They warned me it was going to be graphic, that I should be ready for a chilling sight. Of course, none of that mattered. Just being alive would make her beautiful to me.

Outside the door to the ICU, I motioned the orderly pushing my wheelchair to stop.

"Hold it," I said. "If she can see me, she's going to see me walking. I'm going in under my own power." I got out of the wheelchair and shuffled through the doorway.

It's a good thing the orderly was shadowing me with that wheelchair as I stepped forward, because as soon as I saw Krickitt I fell right back into it. She hadn't needed surgery, but because of her brain injury she had every life support machine in the place plugged into her. She was tied down to the table, straining against the straps and flailing around with seizures. Her eyes and lips were still black, her whole body swollen like a balloon, her head the size of a basketball. There were tubes coming out of her mouth and nose and from underneath the sheets, and IV lines going in both arms and one foot. She had a probe called a camino bolt drilled into her head to measure the pressure between the brain and the skull, with wires coming out of her scalp and connecting to some of the monitors that literally filled the room.

I knew she was woozy from the sedatives and couldn't talk because of all the tubes, but I was desperate to establish some sort of two-way communication.

I got up out of the wheelchair and grabbed Krickitt's hand.

"It's me, babe," I said softly. "If you can hear me, squeeze my hand." We didn't know then that the cool, white hand I held so gingerly was broken too. There was no reaction in her face, no expression of any kind.

But she squeezed.

Krickitt was still in there. Somewhere under all those wires and brokenness the flame of that precious spirit still flickered. It was the first sign of life that we didn't need a machine to understand. *Praise God in his holiness. Praise him in the firmament of his power.*

From the doctors' point of view, though, Krickitt was still much more likely to die than to live. Visiting hours in the intensive care recovery area were strictly limited—only immediate family and only for thirty minutes at a time. Yet the doctors let us all come and go whenever we wanted to. We hadn't heard them tell the staff to let anybody in who wanted to come, since the patient would be dead within hours anyway.

A few minutes after I got to Krickitt's room, her parents and her brother, Jamey, arrived from Phoenix. Dad had picked them up at the Albuquerque terminal, and the three of them came straight up to the ICU. They had spent the endless, agonizing hours of that night packing, crying, and praying for a miracle. But here, Gus and Mary Pappas were incredibly calm, even at the sight of their daughter covered with tubes and wires, her face distorted almost beyond recognition.

My brother Kelly arrived from Roswell. He had been level-headed enough to wait until after sunrise to make the trip when the roads had thawed. Now the family circle was complete.

As the day wore on, we spent a lot of time with the doctors learning exactly what Krickitt's problem was. Actually there were two problems, and one made the other more serious. The first and most dangerous thing was the swelling in her brain. Swelling constricted the flow of blood to her brain cells, and they were starved for the nutrients and oxygen that the blood normally brought in. The second thing was that her blood pressure was dangerously low. Even without any other complications, low pressure would have reduced the blood flow to the organs, especially the brain, eventually damaging it due to lack of oxygen. Swelling plus low blood pressure was a double whammy—constricted blood vessels and weaker blood flow.

Since she had lived this long already, the doctors were beginning to think she might survive after all. Earlier in the morning she had wiggled her fingers and toes, the first sign we'd had that she wasn't paralyzed. Still, they said, every minute the brain had insufficient oxygen increased the chances she would be permanently affected. The brain pressure had gone down for awhile, but spiked up again without warning. They estimated it would take as long as twenty-four hours, and possibly forty-eight, for the swelling to go back down and the oxygen supply to be completely restored.

By that time, if she were still alive, she'd spend the rest of her life a vegetable.

The nurses had taught us how to read the various monitors in the room and what they all meant. We knew what to look for and spent the next part of the day watching the numbers go up and down. Fifteen, they said, was a good pressure reading; higher values were bad, and Krickitt's was up in the mid-50s. Nothing in the world makes you feel so helpless. One number means life, another means death, and you feel like there's nothing you can do but sit and watch.

In all the shock and exhaustion of the day, it took a few minutes for us to remember that we weren't really helpless at all. We'd forgotten that God's miracles are never more than a prayer away. It's true that prayers aren't always answered the way we want, but we hadn't even made the effort in any organized way to bring our need before him.

Along with Mary and Gus, Curtis and Wendy Jones, and a few other friends who had heard the news and come to be with us, Jamey and I went to a small, sparsely furnished chapel nearby and prayed specifically for the pressure on Krickitt's brain to go down. The doctor had said it would be at least twenty-four hours, and by then it would be too late. We prayed for a miracle, asking God to relieve the pressure in time to save her. Jamey, who was with Campus Crusade for Christ at the University of California at Irvine, led us in an impromptu prayer service. He had a special measure of love and grace in his voice as he took his turn praying aloud.

"God, you've said that if we come to you in prayer, you would hear us and grant our request. We ask you to touch Krickitt with your healing hand so that the pressure on her brain will go down. . . ."

Others were praying for her too. Krick's friend Lisa Eberly contacted old college friends and coworkers in California and asked them to lift up Krickitt as a special Thanksgiving Day prayer. Jamey's wife, Gretchen, expecting a baby and staying with her parents in Scottsdale, Arizona, on her doctor's orders, called a network of Campus Crusade staffers and asked them to pray for a healing miracle. They called others in turn, and had a prayer chain by the end of the day that reached all the way to Russia.

After about twenty minutes in the chapel, we went back to the ICU. Automatically my eyes went to the readouts on the monitors we had been watching so long. The numbers were better. I could tell that the pressure on Krickitt's brain was going down. Nurses were in and out of the room every few minutes, and the next time nurse Sherry Kenna came in and looked at the reading, she called for a doctor because she was afraid the monitor probe had slipped out of place. The doctor checked the probe, but it was fine.

Though the brain pressure continued to lessen, Krickitt's blood pressure was still critically low. As word of the accident got out, more and more friends started calling the hospital to check on Krickitt and offer their prayers. The switchboard got so busy the receptionist eventually rerouted incoming ICU calls directly to the waiting room telephone. Still more friends arrived from church, along with our pastor, Fred Maldonado, and all of us went to the chapel again to pray specifically that her blood pressure would go up.

We got back to the room and looked at the monitor. Her blood pressure was on a steady rise. Nurse Kenna came in to check her condition again. When she saw the blood pressure reading, her jaw dropped. She looked at me and pointed to the readout, then hesitated for a long second like she couldn't get the words out.

"Look at that pressure," she said finally. We were. We couldn't take our eyes off of it. Headed straight toward the normal range.

Krickitt gradually became more alert. In the helicopter twelve hours earlier, her heart rate had careened back and forth between 50 and 170 beats a minutes. Just six hours after that she was facing life in a vegetative state. Now her vital signs were approaching normal, and obviously she was going to have at least some of her functions back.

I spent the next few days trying to rest up and get some of my own strength back. I walked from my room down to Krickitt's several times a day, taking it slow, leaning against the wall in the hallway as I went, since I still couldn't stand up straight on account of my ribs and back. Krickitt continued to improve, and the Monday after Thanksgiving, five days after the accident, she was moved from the ICU to acute care and taken off life support.

Technically she was still in a coma. (Up until that time I thought people in a coma were unconscious, period. At least that's the way they always were on TV. The real-world medical definition is different, though. There are fifteen separate levels of coma, and the least serious ones include states where the patient is alert enough to move around and talk a little.) She slept almost around the clock, but with the life support tubes out of her throat I knew she could finally talk to me. I had been desperate for the sound of her voice ever since I screamed for her in the seconds after the wreck. There were so many times when I thought I'd never hear it again. I dreamed she was talking to me—a sound like music, refreshing and renewing like water in the desert.

The doctor said I could feed her ice chips. I touched a small piece to her lips, and she ate it from my fingers. Her lips weren't so black anymore. They were very pale and dry, but I could feel their warmth and the warmth of her breath on my fingertips.

I fed her another piece, and another one. I put my face inches from hers.

"I love you, Krickitt," I said softly.

"I love you too."

It was an absolute miracle. It was what I wanted to hear more than anything in the world. Krickitt was still in there. Still knew me. Still loved me. *Till death do us part.*

Chapter 3

I'M NOT MARRIED

It didn't matter to me that the doctors thought Krickitt's answer was just a reflexive response, and that she really didn't understand what either one of us was saying. Maybe they were right from a medical standpoint, but I felt a connection that gave me hope anyway. Her pressure readings returning to normal were the first sign we'd had that her condition had stopped getting worse and started getting better. Her words were another step on the road back for us.

There was still no way to know how fully she would recover. When her eyes were open, they were frozen in a stare like doll's eyes. She looked at things without seeming to recognize them and acted like she couldn't figure out what was going on. Part of the short-term solution was strictly low-tech. Her dad asked if anyone had taken her contact lenses out. They had, and somebody then had the brainstorm that we should put her glasses on her. It was like flipping a switch. All of a sudden she was a lot more plugged in during the few minutes at a time she was awake. The first thing she saw was a plate of Jell-O across the room, and it animated her more than anything else we'd tried. She began to focus more on me when I talked to her. It was a tiny victory, but it still moved us closer to the day when I would have my Krickitt home again.

Over the next few days she started sitting up, then standing, then taking a few shuffling steps across the room and back. She hardly lifted her feet off the floor, and had me on one side and an attendant on the other. It was hard to watch a two-time academic All-American gymnast struggle so much to put one foot in front of the other. What it meant, though, was that she was restoring at least enough brain function that she wouldn't be bedridden the rest of her life. It was a sign that her balance and coordination would come back enough so she could walk again one day.

I praised her for every step. When I talked, she turned her head to look at me now.

"I love you, Krickitt."

"I love you too."

Still no inflection in her voice or expression on her face. I stared deep into her eyes, daring at last to look for the old Krickitt in there somewhere. But I didn't see her yet.

She started eating pudding and other soft foods. She couldn't feed herself, so I came at mealtime to feed her. She sat propped up in the bed, hands limp at her side. When I held the spoon up to her mouth, she opened it to take a bite. She looked at me sometimes, or at the food, but spent most of the time staring straight ahead at the wall on the other side of the room.

She still had no control over her body functions, so the nurse had put an adult diaper on her. When I was with her and there was a need, I changed it for her. In a way it sounds disgusting, but it was one of the few things I could do to show her how much I cared for her and wanted to help her and be with her. It was something I could do that made her comfortable. Her needs had been reduced to the most basic needs of life. And if that was what she needed, that's what I wanted to give her.

Krickitt's doctors had been talking about where to send her for the long rehabilitation program we had ahead of us. Restoring brain-injured people to their maximum potential is an intense, highly specialized, expensive process, and they wanted to send her wherever she would have the best chance for rebuilding her life. The good news was that one of the best possible places, Barrow Neurological Institute, was at St. Joseph's Hospital in Phoenix, where Krickitt's parents lived. The bad news, the social worker warned us, was that our HMO was unlikely to allow Krickitt to be moved out of New Mexico for rehab.

"Fine," I said. "Then they can pay for her parents and me to move to Albuquerque and pay our rent as long as we're here." No doubt the social worker was a lot more diplomatic than that, because in spite of her dire predictions, our insurance carrier gave us permission to go out of state right away. We still had to have $1,500 cash for an air ambulance, which supposedly would be refunded after all the insurance papers were filed. The day of the flight, Gus dashed over to the bank just before it closed and got a cashier's check.

It looked for some reason like we weren't going to be able to get into Barrow, so they arranged for Krickitt to be admitted to a head injury rehab program called Rehab Without Walls, which had been started in Mesa by doctors from Barrow. Ten days after the accident, Krickitt and I, along with two medical attendants, boarded an air ambulance for Mesa. Gus and Mary drove my pickup from Albuquerque to meet us there.

After the plane landed, I walked to the terminal for a minute and saw a cat on the way back. Krickitt adores cats, and I thought she might like to pet this one. I picked it up and was carrying it in my arms, looking down at it as I walked, and ran right into the wing of the air ambulance. It knocked me flat on my back, which hurt all the time anyway, and didn't do my other broken bones any good either. Everybody gathered round and lifted me back onto my feet. I felt silly for being so careless, and Krick never did get to hold the cat.

The ambulance driver met us and asked us why we'd landed in Mesa since it was an hour away from the hospital. His instructions were to take us to Barrow in Phoenix. It took a little while to get the story straight, but while we were in the air, somebody realized that Rehab Without Walls was an outpatient clinic—a place for patients who were a lot further along in their recovery than Krickitt was, or not as seriously injured. Alerted to the problem, Rehab Without Walls had then called Barrow and explained to them that Krickitt and I were already on our way to Arizona, needed their higher degree of specialized care, and asked them to admit her. They quickly agreed.

What an answer to prayer! Unaware of the change in plans, Krickitt's parents arrived in Mesa to meet us, and ended up spending lots of time on the phone to Rehab Without Walls and Barrow before finally learning we had been admitted to Barrow after all.

We got to Barrow Neurological Institute late that afternoon. We brought all kinds of X-rays, CAT scans, and other things with us, but the doctor we met explained that they did all their own tests. He introduced himself as the neuropsychologist in charge at Barrow and seemed supremely confident and reassuring.

True to his word, the staff whisked Krickitt off for tests. Later, after we'd gotten her settled in her room, a doctor came in who introduced himself as Dr. Singh's associate. Dr. Singh would be Krick's doctor, the associate explained, and would meet her for the first time the following Monday morning. The associate was jovial, friendly, reassuring, and all the things you want a doctor to be. He was also easy to spot, since he was usually the only one in the room with a turban. It was Friday; we would have the weekend to get used to the surroundings, then Krickitt's therapy would start Monday morning.

I had been in and out of the hospital as a patient a total of six times in Gallup and Albuquerque, yet I'd never been admitted overnight because I couldn't stand to be away from Krickitt. I was petrified that she would die when I was away, even though she was continuing to improve a little bit at a time. What little sleeping I did was with my eyes literally wide open, never truly able to relax.

I moved in with Krickitt's parents in Phoenix with the idea of staying as long as she was in rehab. My broken bones were on the mend, and the surgeons in Albuquerque had repaired my ear and nose—in a few months no one would be able to tell I'd ever injured them. The biggest physical problem was my back. I slept on the floor to try to get comfortable, but nothing seemed to work. Though the cuts from the sunroof glass were healing, I had searing nerve pains shooting up and down my spine, never knowing when they would come or how long they would last.

Another great unknown was how long I'd be in Phoenix. Over the past ten days I'd hardly thought about my job or any of our responsibilities back home in Las Vegas. Gilbert Sanchez, the president of New Mexico Highlands University and my ultimate boss, had tried to call me at the hospital in Albuquerque when I was still in the ER and finally caught up with me soon after we got to Barrow. I told him what little I could about our situation. There was still so much we didn't know that I had no idea when I'd be back. After Christmas vacation my team would need to start working out and getting in shape, and there were other athletic department responsibilities to deal with, but I hadn't been in touch with anybody, hadn't gotten anybody to take my place, and had more or less left the team in the lurch.

Gilbert was characteristically generous and matter-of-fact. "Take all the time you need," he told me on the phone. "You'll always have a job. We'll get whatever help we need for the department until you get back." He also made me promise to give him weekly updates on Krickitt's condition.

Our friends back at Highlands were already helping us in other ways too, without us even knowing about it. Three cheerleaders moved into our apartment to house-sit. Mike Kloeppel mailed our bills to me. When our landlord heard what happened, he told me not to worry about the rent, just to pay him later if we could, otherwise forget it.

Krickitt's room at Barrow was very plain, with yellowish-tan walls and the usual hospital furniture. The heliport must have been right on top of us, because we heard helicopters coming and going from the roof above us five or six times a day.

In contrast to the commotion the helicopters made, there was a window facing a courtyard full of peaceful-looking flower beds and walkways. Since it was the first week of December, nothing was blooming. But seeing it made me look forward to the time Krickitt and I would be taking walks there together. She had already come so far, and I knew this was one of the best places in the country for the kind of care she needed. Surely it wouldn't be long until we were out there looking at the flowers and talking about going home.

The patients in the rooms around Krickitt were at various stages in their recovery. Some of them had been in car wrecks like she had, and some had suffered strokes or aneurysms. There was a sheriff's officer who had been shot in the line of duty, with a twenty-four-hour guard posted outside his door. There was an attorney who'd had an aneurysm. Next door to us was a patient we soon nicknamed Moaning Lady because she moaned day and night for hours at a time.

For Krickitt's first look at another part of the hospital, a nurse and I wheeled her into the patient cafeteria for lunch on Saturday. It was a ghastly sight. The room was full of carefully attended but severely disabled people shouting, moaning, or mumbling incoherently, some with shaved heads and stapled incisions, waving their arms, drooling, vomiting, or staring blankly into space.

I looked at Krickitt and felt fear in her. We were totally unprepared for this sort of spectacle, and there was no reason on earth why we should have to sit in the middle of all this. "This scares you," I said almost involuntarily, not exactly sure if I'd said it out loud or just thought it.

"Yeah," Krickitt answered, her voice still a raspy whisper after five days with a breathing tube down her throat. The scene penetrated even her hazy consciousness. I hadn't expected her to say anything and felt a burst of joy that even in a place like this God could remind me he's always keeping watch over my life.

We went back to the room, and Krickitt ate her meals there until she could go to the regular cafeteria. When our doctor found out what happened, he assigned us a different therapy support team. That was a good move; none of the family wanted to risk exposing Krickitt—or the rest of us—again to such shocking and depressing reminders of what could happen to head injury patients. Actually, it was somewhat encouraging to see people being treated and improving who were worse off than Krick. But for us in our situation, once was definitely enough.

Over the weekend we learned what sort of schedule Krickitt would be on from day to day. The first session would be occupational therapy, where she would relearn personal skills like getting bathed and dressed. Then she would spend time in speech therapy, where a specialist would identify any speech disability caused by the injury and teach Krickitt how to overcome it.

The third session of the day was physical therapy, where she would work on her hand-eye coordination, balance, and motor skills. The girl who went to Cal State on a full-ride gymnastics scholarship would have to learn to walk again.

After lunch, she would spend the last part of the day working on basic household chores like cooking, vacuuming, and making a bed.

Krickitt was still sleeping most of the time and still disoriented. The first night at Barrow she woke up, tried to get to the bathroom, and ended up getting stuck in the bed rail that had been raised for her protection. Needless to say, she didn't make it to the toilet in time. From then on, someone slept in the room with her every night. Her mom was there every evening for about three weeks straight.

Though she was conscious for short periods, it would be twenty-one days in all after the accident before Krickitt was officially out of her "charted coma." She was still sleeping more than twenty hours a day and still couldn't carry on a conversation more than a minute or two. But the first Monday morning after we arrived, she was supposed to meet Dr. Singh. I got there early to try and wake her gently and help her get ready for the big day ahead. I talked to her and stroked her face, but she stayed sound asleep. I shook her shoulder, and still she didn't budge.

At that moment a man came in, dressed like he'd just stepped out of *GQ* magazine. "Good morning," he beamed, "I'm Dr. Raj Singh." He didn't look anything like I'd expected. No white lab coat, no stethoscope, no clinical aloofness. (Also, unlike his associate, no turban.) He gave me a reassuring handshake, walked to the bed, and leaned over Krickitt. I had been doing my best to bring her to consciousness carefully, but the doctor had a better plan.

"You have to wake up," he said firmly. No response.

"You have to wake up," he repeated with exactly the same inflection. Still nothing.

He reached over and pinched her inside the front collar of her hospital gown. Hard.

Her eyes flew open. "Leave me alone, you —— !" Here she shouted the locker room word for the place where the person meets the saddle and the sun never shines.

Now that he had her undivided attention, he told her to wiggle her right hand. She did. He told her to wiggle her left foot, and she did. The doctor looked at me with a huge grin on his face. "She will do well," he said confidently. Within the hour she was down the hall working on her first occupational therapy lesson.

Since the accident I had thought about Krickitt every minute of the day. I was still awestruck at the fact that her life had been spared. My mom and dad had seen our car at the wrecking yard in Gallup. They'd gone there to look for my wallet and found it still in the back seat. The car was completely crushed, Dad said, the inside covered with blood and hair.

With Krickitt out of immediate danger, I could turn to filing insurance claims and organizing the medical paperwork that was already starting to stack up. During our first days at Barrow, when
Krickitt was still in a coma, a call came for her from one of the emergency equipment providers, wondering when they might expect
their check.

The taste of food was one of the few pleasures Krick could appre-
ciate. Mealtime became a treat for both of us—for her because she
enjoyed eating, and for me because it was one of the times in the day
when she was the most animated. Soon she was eating on her own,
and her favorite food was yogurt. We went to the hospital cafeteria
after her physical therapy class. She was talking more and seemed
more plugged in during our conversations.

Some of Krickitt's friends had come to visit her while we were still
in Albuquerque, and one special friend had been anxious to see her
but couldn't come until now. Lisa Eberly was Krickitt's roommate
when Krickitt and I met, and she had been in our wedding. Lisa was
the one who kept calling Gus and Mary at home the night of the accident until they got back from their basketball game. She and Megan
Almquist, another roommate who had also been Krickitt's maid of
honor, flew in from California, and Mary picked them up at the airport. Other old friends of Krickitt's came, too, and decorated her hospital room with Christmas lights and a little tree. Adding all the flowers and cards on display, she had the most colorful room on the floor.

By the time Lisa and Megan came, Krickitt looked a whole lot better than she had in the Albuquerque ICU, but she was still a very seriously injured, very banged-up young woman. Because she was so
improved, and since I saw her every day, I didn't think about how
somebody who hadn't seen her since the wreck might react.

So I hadn't said anything to prepare Lisa for the sight of Krickitt with her head partially shaved, her zombie-like stare, and the general look of a person who has been more or less unconscious for three weeks. Lisa came bounding into the room, took one good, long look at Krickitt, and started trembling. She opened her mouth but no words came out. I escorted her to a private family meeting room down the hall and we both had a good cry.

Like all the thoughtful friends who came to see us, Lisa was almost like a visitor from another planet. She was from a world where people got up, had breakfast, went to work, watched TV, ate in restaurants, read magazines, got their hair cut, and did all the other little normal everyday things of life without even thinking about them. My world had become a world of doctors, hospitals, hospital food, therapy, living with my in-laws, taking calls from collection agencies about medical bills, making calls to our insurance company, and spending as much time as I could with Krickitt. My job, my team, my friends, my married life—all that was some kind of distant daydream.

I was beginning to wonder if I could keep everything pasted together. My back still hurt all the time, and I was taking heavy-duty painkillers to get me through the day. (Krickitt's parents even hid my car keys for awhile, fearful I'd get woozy behind the wheel.) Then at night I thought about all the things that might happen to Krickitt when I wasn't there to help her. I became terrified that somehow she would die in her sleep. I lay awake all night dreading what would happen, afraid the phone would ring any second and it would be the hospital telling me Krickitt was dead.

Sometimes I'd drift away to happy thoughts or funny things that had happened over the past three weeks. One day my brother Kirk came to see me in Phoenix, and we went to an amusement park and rode the roller coaster. My ribs were still taped up, and by the end of the ride I was in agony. When it was finally over he said, "Want to ride again?" And I said, "Yeah, right, you idiot. I can't believe you talked me into going on it to begin with!"

But then I'd start thinking of Krickitt in the hospital bed, in the dark, imagining her there asleep, taking one slow breath after another. Would that breath be the last one? Or that one? Or that?

Then I'd wonder what Krickitt would be like when all this was over. We hadn't even been married three months—we had barely started our life together. We'd had a fantastic wedding ceremony and a honeymoon in Hawaii. Then we'd moved into our apartment in Las Vegas, New Mexico, unpacked, I'd started the new school year coaching at Highlands, and that was it—the sum total of our married life. Would Krickitt ever be the same person as the Krickitt I married? Could she have a career? Could she have children?

All these thoughts tumbled around in my head night after night until the dark in my borrowed bedroom turned to gray ahead of the approaching sunrise. Then I got up, got dressed, and headed for another day at Barrow.

After only a short while at Barrow, Krickitt was obviously improving. She seemed stronger, more alert, and more talkative every morning. The zombie stare was nearly gone and she interacted more naturally with whoever was speaking to her.

The therapists were still being very careful with her, having her move slowly, working simple puzzles, walking with a harness. Now that she could understand them and answer questions, they had also started assessing her memory and other mental skills. She sounded like a little girl when she answered them, speaking in a few one- and two-syllable words after long pauses for concentrating on what she would say, shaping the words slowly and carefully as though they felt unfamiliar.

It was a Tuesday, and Krickitt was talking with a therapist who was probing carefully for what Krickitt could remember. I was sitting at the table with them. Her "I love you" had been the first sign things were getting back to normal. Now I was ready for even bigger proof. I wanted my wife back.

"Krickitt," the therapist said in that quiet-but-you-better-pay-attention voice they have, "Krickitt, do you know where you are?"

Krickitt thought for a minute. "Phoenix."

"Right. That's great, Krickitt. Now, do you know what year it is?"

Another pause. "1965." She was born in 1969. *A little setback— nothing to worry about.*

"Krickitt, who's the president?"

"Nixon." She was five presidents off, but she had the right one for the date she'd picked.

"Krickitt, who's your mother? Who's your mom?"

"Mary." Less hesitation this time, though still no expression. *Now we're getting somewhere. Thank you, God!*

"That's right, Krickitt, excellent. Mary. Now Krickitt, who's your father?"

"Gus."

"Gus. That's right, Krickitt. Very good."

"Krickitt, who's your husband?"

A pause. She looked into my eyes. Still no expression. She looked back at the therapist.

"Krickitt, who's your husband?"

She looked at me again and back at the therapist. My heart was pounding so hard I was sure everybody in the room could hear it. I was desperate to hear her say my name.

"I'm not married."

God, no.

"Krickitt, who's your husband?"

She wrinkled her brow. "Todd?" It came out as a question, not an answer.

Todd? An old boyfriend from California. Please, God, help her!

"Think, Krickitt. Who's your husband?

"I told you. I'm not married."

Chapter 4

KRICKITT'S DIARY 1—
"But I say to the unmarried . . . ."

THIS DIARY BELONGS TO:
Krisxan Pappas

*To my
Jesus; my Lord,
my life, my God, and my
bright shining Light.
I love you.*

5/30/92

Graduation Day

To my Jesus:

I love you so much, and I thank you for how merciful you have been w/me, loving, caring, and so generous. Thanks for my college scholarship, thanks for so many awesome years at Cal State, some where I really strayed from your side, but many where I learned what it meant to walk with you.

Today was graduation day from CSUF. It was so fun. I grad. w/ honors, and that is only because of you Lord. I give you all of the credit. You truly are the one to be praised... May your light shine through the darkness, dear God. Please allow me to be a bold witness for you. Thanks for everything. Please open my heart & eyes to see your beauty & specialness. You're the best friend I have—I love you, Lord.

—KP

1 Thess 5:24 "Faithful is He who calls you, and He also will bring it to pass."

6/7/92

Lord Jesus,

I thank you for being so patient w/ me, God. I thank you for my job at Jammin' Sportswear. I really like it. I put it completely in your hands and ask that you help me not to get boastful, but to only boast in you. I put all of my sales in your hands, and pray you will help me. I know I can't do it w/out your help. Help me to be a hard worker, but not that I forget about what is truly important.

Today was a long day, but I feel good about working hard. I realize that it is all in vain if I'm not doing it for you. I pray for your continued help. Most of all, open the hearts of the people I work with so I can be a real light. I pray you will show me if anyone is a Christian there. I pray that you will open up doors for me to share. Help me to be bold & stand up for you.

—KP

6/12/92

Dear Lord,

How sweet you are and your word is to my ears. I love you so much and know that only you can bring me joy and happiness. I lift my hand and eyes to you. Forgive me of my sin. Wash me clean, God. Forgive me when my heart is unpure, or I have evil in my heart. I want to have motives and desires that are from you. I pray that I will be em-powered by your Holy Spirit today. Let me be an example God. Please open the doors for me to be bold & share w/ people there....Help me to find my security in you, Lord, & my deep deep needs met by you. I love you—protect me dear Jesus

—KP

6/12/92 [second entry]

Lord Jesus,

Today has been a really nice & relaxing day. We rode my bike to the beach & laid out. I'm on a date with you, Father. Right now I'm sitting in my beach chair watching your sun go down for the night. I thank you for all of the joy you have restored to me. I feel so good right now—so content. I know my life & my future are in your hands. I trust you, Lord, that you will guide & direct me in the ways I should go.

Sometimes I wonder where you are going to call me to. Whoever's wife I will be, I pray that you continue to prepare me to be the godly woman for my husband. The one you would be so proud of, Lord Jesus. Prepare my husband for me too, Lord. Draw us both ever so close to you. Whoever he is, I know I can offer him a lot, because you have made me a really neat Christian gal. I have seen so many changes in my life it blows me away. Thank you. Show my heart what you desire. I want to stay so pure God. I'm putting my trust in you.

I took a picture of the sunset because this is our date together. Please continue to fill me w/ your love & your will be done. May your Spirit continue to work in my heart & life & may I bear your fruits. I love you Lord.

—Krickitt/Krisxan

6/15/92

Dear Jesus,

Thank you for a day that shows me that I must rely on your strength. I know when I am at work I am there to serve you. Give me strength & motivation. Thank you for joy—for being happy w/ who I am. Lord I do want to go to the singles group Thurs. I am ready to settle down w/ my husband. Provide me people to go out w/ if that's your will. I want someone who will be crazy for me—I don't see that so far. It may occur—it may not.

I'm looking forward to meeting other people my same age & direction. God, I put this in your hands. Guard my heart because I have no idea where you are leading all of this. You know my heart & my desires. I desire godliness & openness & communication. Help me to trust you & place everything in your hands. Let me have pure motives, Lord. I feel it will be good for me to see how it is to talk to other guys my age w/ my same focus. Help me to be the godly woman you desire of me. Help me be a woman of integrity.

—KP

6/20/92

Father God,

I thank you truly for who you are. For being my strength, comfort, & shield. You have given me so much & I give to you so little. I ask for your continued guidance in my life. Do you have someone for me? No need for me to stress. I know you know my desires. I want to delight myself in you, God. Please be my strength & comfort.

Lord, I won't pretend I have it all together because it's obvious I don't. I won't pretend I don't look at guys & wonder what they are like because I have. I have to say I met one guy who knows Jamey & Gretchen that seemed really nice—maybe because he was real friendly & introduced himself to me & he's cute & sold out for God most likely. Who knows? All I know is that you know my needs & desires. I place my future in your hands.

It's been neat to see you working in my life. Help me to mature like you. Please develop into me the godly qualities you want me to have as a wife some day. Father, give me wisdom and guidance. Help me—guide me—show me—fill me. —Krisxan

7/9/92

Lord,

It's been good to see you working in my life and using me in the lives of other people. At times I don't see it, but then I get a reminder of how much you love me & have done in my life. I rest easy in you today, knowing that you are totally in control. Especially at work, you are so awesome and I know you understand me and know my need. God, I love you and want to fall more in love w/ you day by day. I don't want to fear love and be afraid of it, dear Jesus. I don't want to put up walls, but I want to rest in you, knowing you are going to protect my heart.

I want to have perfect love like you, Lord. I know that only through you can I have such a thing.

—KP

7/11/92

Father—

I express to you right now my feelings, my fears, my worries, my burdens, my thoughts. I know we have talked through a lot of them, but I feel I need to *take the time and express them to you. Lord Jesus, I know you hear me right now, even though you feel kind of distant. I know you are really working in my situation, and that, dear Jesus, is such a good feeling.*

I guess I have so many dreams and desires, Lord. I desire to be a wife to someone someday. I want to be the jewel in his life, next to you. I want him to be proud to say this is my wife Krisxan. I desire to be serving you with your desire. I want to be an encouragement to others and an example of a godly wife & godly woman. I pray that you are making me that girl right now. Please instill in me the qualities that you want. I desire righteousness & holiness. I often think I would love to be a pastor's wife, so where does that dream & desire take me? I know that you know how you can use me for the furthering of your kingdom. I like to depend on you God, and I see right now how I do need to depend on you.

Well, God, these are my deepest, most precious thoughts. Please make my heart be your desires. It's wild, because if someone w/ quality asked me out, I

*would love to go out! Father, I lay this at your feet &
thanks for protecting my heart.*

*Thanks so much for being my comforter, my
healer, my peace. I can see you really working in
my heart & lifting it off of the ground. It's been really nice to be able to lean on you, Father God. I
know you are in control of my life. I know you see
me seeking you. Thanks for really seeing my desires and allowing them to be yours. Help me to be
patient & focus on you, dear Jesus. I'm trusting you,
God, w/ my future. Give me vision. Guide me,
Father. Help me to trust you & seek your face continually. I can't do anything w/ out you.*

—Love, Krisxan

7/16/92

Lord Jesus—

*I thank you for hope & peace. Thanks for a full-
ness in my heart when I don't even know why it's
there. Thanks for joy in the midst of trial.*

*Please help me to trust you & know you are
preparing my husband for me, God. He's awesome—*

I'm sure. You know my devotion to you & the man I need must have that same devotion.

Please guide & direct my path, Lord. Protect my heart. Guide me day by day, hour by hour, minute by minute. You truly are my Rock, my salvation and of course, my redeemer & my Savior. Fill me w/ <u>your</u> joy & Spirit. Let's begin w/ today. Thanks, Lord.

—Krickitt

7/19/92

Precious Jesus,

I know you are in control of my life & that feels good. I thought I'd see a certain guy today, but I didn't. Thanks for not allowing it to dictate my attitude. I know you have someone great in store for me. I place my life in your hands, knowing that you are continually preparing me for my husband & ministry. Give me vision, direction. Show me what you desire for me & for me to do. May I rest in you & at your feet. Lord, take all of me.

I know you are in control, and especially when it comes to my love life. I feel so ready to give my heart and hand to someone, but not if they can't take it. Keep me patient and protected in your love. I know you are preparing my husband for me right now.

—Krisxan

7/24/92

Dear Lord,

Thank you for contentment in my heart. I see you every day taking my hand and walking me down a path to serve you. My heart lays heavy some days. I long for a loving relationship. I know Lord as my love relationship with you grows, in time, you will provide me with one that will be so much more than I could ever expect. One that will be challenging & growing. I want my man to be attracted to my inner beauty that comes from you. Help me to rest in you, knowing that you will guide me into the relationship you desire me to be in.

I am ready to give myself to my man, but you have to prepare him. Lord, be with my husband right now. Draw him close to you. Make him long for our relationship. Hold him close, give him great *fellowship & accountability. Help me to be more like you, Lord. Change me Father—continually. I love you God—let me be your witness.*

—Krisxan

8/16/92

Lord,

Please help me be patient. I long to meet my hus-band & grow with him. Prepare him for me, God. I know you desire for me more than I can imagine. Satisfy my soul with you. You truly are my heart's delight. You can & promise to meet my deepest needs. Thanks for giving me pure joy on this morn-ing. I thank you for my new roomies Lisa & Megan. Please prepare us all to live with one an-other. Thanks for fellowship and friends that really care.

8/22/92

Romans 8:26–28

"And in the same way the Spirit also helps our weakness; for we do not know how to pray as we should, but the Spirit Himself intercedes for us with

groanings too deep for words; and He who searches the hearts knows what the mind of the Spirit is, because he intercedes according to the will of God. And we know that God causes all things to work together for good to those who love God, to those who are called according to His purpose."

8/29/92

Dear Jesus—

I look back on this summer and I feel so good about it. I can see how you really used me this summer here in Fullerton. It's a really good feeling. I pray that you would continue to do that.

Please continue to work in me and show me what ministry you want me to do. Please burden my heart in the direction you want me to go. Please continue to mold me into the godly woman you desire me to be. Also prepare me to be the wife you want me to be for my husband. I pray for him too— that you would allow us to begin growing in our relationship. I know you want to give me the desires of my heart. I want to meet my husband. Help me to be patient. God, I plead with you, have mercy—I *feel I have waited patiently and been obedient. I want you to know how I feel, but I know ultimately it will be your timing. Help me be content with that, and content with you.*

Please Lord, I put these requests in your hands, totally trusting you with them, knowing if I delight myself in you, you will give me the desires of my heart. I love you, Lord. Thanks for all of my blessings.

—Krisxan

8/30/92

. . . I want a husband who is sold out for you, honest, sincere, trustworthy, funny, goofy, yet serious, thoughtful, romantic, likes the ocean, likes to dance & be crazy, plays guitar, is easygoing, makes me feel adored, has good communication and social skills, has a good family, attractive, athletic, loving, open, real, spirit-filled, likes my family, aspires to grow with me and spend time with me, a spiritual leader, will look me in the eye.

God, I trust you with my heart, with my future husband, and future plans. Oh Lord, I know you

are preparing me for my mate, even as we speak. I can rest in that and trust you in that. Thanks for a real feeling of joy, happiness, and excitement today.
   —KP
   I am ready to get on with this.

9/9/92
God,
   Please be with my husband and prepare him for you today & our marriage & courtship. May I meet him soon. Please make us the godly people you desire us to be.
   May my heart be steadfast for you, my Jesus.
   —KP

9/14/92
   —Philippians 4:6 "Be anxious for nothing, but in everything by prayer and supplication with thanksgiving let your requests be made known to God. And the peace of God, which surpasses all comprehension, shall guard your hearts and your minds in Christ Jesus."

9/22/92

Lord Jesus—

I desire so much to be in ministry and with my husband. These dreams & desires I have are so real and so true, Lord! Do you see them, I often wonder? But yes, I know you do. Will my day ever come? I often wonder and ask. But of course it will. I pray for my husband wherever he might be, that you would prepare us for one another. Help me to be the woman of God he has always dreamed of. May he treat me the way I deserve & you deserve. May we glorify you in our marriage & with our children. May our love for you continue to grow & may I be satisfied with you alone, Lord. I know you fill my every part. You make me happy & you make me secure. I love you, Lord. Thanks for everything. Please help me to glorify you tomorrow.

—KP

11/19/92

Dear Jesus,

I pray for my own scheming nature, that if it is apparent, please show me. Oh Lord, how I do pray for my husband. Please bring him soon, so we can grow together in our relationship with one another & our relationship with you. I just pray that it will be so apparent for both of us—that we will be like a glove. I pray that we would find each other exciting & refreshing, but most of all encourage each other. I desire so bad to be a wife—a godly example. Lord, I pray for both of us to continue to seek you & be ready for one another. It excites me so much.

Lord Jesus, please be with me today & lift me up & fill me with your joy, peace, patience, kindness, goodness, & self-control. I love you, Lord.

—Krisxan

12/15/92

1 Corinthians 7:3 "Let the husband fulfill his duty to his wife, and likewise also the wife to her husband."

Husbands and wives need to learn how to give and take in their relationship. I see it as a two-way street. When I think of my duties as a wife, I feel like I need to be very supportive and encouraging of my husband. I want to be supportive to him, an

*ear always open and arms always ready to em-
brace him when he walks through the door. I want
to keep his home clean & tidy and myself looking
nice for him. I want to be the communicative friend
and lover that he deserves and needs. I want to
treat him with respect and never fail to show him
how much I love him. I want the Lord to be the center of our household. I pray that I could be the spiritual wife that he needs, full of wisdom and knowledge, and the example my children can model. I
pray that our marriage will be an example to others—beginning at courtship through eternity.*

*I pray for my husband right now. I pray that
you would continue to develop in him the qualities
you desire. Please put many Christians in his life
for accountability and growth. Make him sweet as
honey—I pray that our hearts will begin growing towards one another. I pray that our paths would
begin to cross, and our friendship would begin to
develop. I desire so much to begin that relationship
growing together as one. I pray that you would
begin preparing me to be the wife my husband*

needs, show me areas that I need to grow in. I pray that you would continually mold me.

Continue to guide my friendships—I pray that the friendships you desire me to have would just blossom. May your Holy Spirit be working mightily.

Keep me patient while my friends around me are getting married—those that are younger than me. It can be a little frustrating as their dreams are being fulfilled, while even though I'm taking the right path, mine are at a standstill. I know that I must be patient, and at your perfect timing my desires will be delighted by you. Guide my paths and keep me focused on you—I love you & need you, Lord.

—Krisxan

12/17/92

1 Corinthians 7:8

"But I say to the unmarried and to widows that it is good for them if they remain even as I."

This is a hard passage for me to read because I feel like it conflicts so much with what my heart desires. I do see that being single can be used of the Lord and it is seen as good in the sight of the Lord. It is something that I accept every day and am thankful for. My heart just aches with delight at the thought of holding my children & being the best wife to a man. I know that you desire to use me for your glory, and my heart patters at the thought of being a witness in my marriage. I pray as I am single that you would help me to be content and focus on <u>Christ.</u> I know you desire to use me, Lord. Guide my paths.

—KP

12/19/92

1 Corinthians 7:32, 34

"One who is unmarried is concerned about the things of the Lord, how he may please the Lord . . . And the woman who is unmarried, and the virgin, is concerned about the things of the Lord, that she may be holy both in body and spirit."

These are really hard words for me to read, Lord. I guess it's because it seems to go against some of my wishes to be a supportive, encouraging wife &

mother someday. I'm praying by faith that the "someday" will come. But it's true, I do need to give you all of the time & devotion you need. I pray, Lord, that I would be concerned of the things that please you. May I continue to live and glorify you with my actions. I ask for forgiveness. I feel as though I have been really selfish lately and unmotivated. Please forgive me, Lord. Make me like you, Lord, make me like you.

I am an unmarried virgin and know that is so precious in your sight. May you continue to make me holy both in body & spirit. Keep me pure & my thoughts free from lust. May your Holy Spirit really dwell within me. I want undistracted devotion to you, Lord. Sometimes I feel as though if I were married I would be using my gifts to the fullest. Maybe that is an excuse. You know what is best for me & I trust you. You never said we wouldn't suffer walking your walk. I know all is well with it. I praise your name. I praise you for all of your beauty that lies around me. I thank you for who you are. Thank you, my Savior, for dying for me—thank you for this Christmas, that you my Savior chose to be born a baby, so I could live with you.

May you continue to guide my heart & make my desires yours. Thank you, Jesus—may you continue to use me & open my heart to the lost. Give me boldness & that fire for you once again. I can't wait to see how you bring my husband into my life. May my focus be on you. Keep me patient. Help me to keep my eyes on you—the author & perfector of my faith. Make me more like you each day, Lord. I need you so much. In your holy name.

—Krisxan

January 1, 1993

Lord,

Wow, it's a new year—and I do dedicate it to you. I give you my life, please use me for your glory. It scares me to say that because I fear a bad thing will happen. I pray this year I would meet my husband if it is your will. I pray for an on-fire heart. I pray for good & challenging fellowship.

I have sought you more & spent more time with you & you have been <u>so silent</u> this year—especially

these past months. Please don't let me fall down—
even physical struggles I have. I long to give myself
completely to someone—I have faith <u>some</u> <u>day</u> this
will happen and I can be a wife & mom.

Please burden my heart, Lord. I confess my long-
ing to release the desires within me. Forgive me.
Forgive me for putting you aside. It's been a real
struggle because I haven't seen a big difference
lately. I know my fruits are fuller when I am with
you. Lord, forgive me of my impatience, impure
thoughts, selfishness. Make me like you, Lord. Help
me be more consistent in my prayer life—I get so
overwhelmed.

Please be with me this new year. My heart is
yours.

—Love, Krisxan

Chapter 5

LEAVE ME ALONE

I told you. I'm not married." What she said was no worse than the matter-of-fact way she said it. I looked deep into her eyes, praying for even the slightest hint of recognition. But she stared back at me, a stranger. Although I had been with her since the accident practically every minute she was awake, and she recognized me when I came in the door and answered back when I spoke to her, this was the first moment it hit me that she had absolutely no idea who I was.

I felt a prickly sensation all over and a strange lightness as the adrenaline rush came—part of the built-up excitement and anticipation of this instant when the curtain would be lifted, the cobwebs torn away, and I would know I had my wife back. But instead of elation, the moment only fueled my shock and disappointment. I staggered out of Krickitt's room into the hall, hammering the wall with my fist like a lunatic. Even the searing pain of the broken hand I was pounding with—still in a soft cast—couldn't penetrate my rage.

As fierce as my reaction was, the whole thing was over in a minute or two. I walked back into the room, spent and defeated, and stood beside Krickitt's bed. She looked up at me without anger or curiosity, like she was ready for another question or for me to tell her something. I opened my mouth but couldn't get any words to come out.

Over the next few days as I went back and forth between Barrow and the Pappas house, I prayed for a new direction in my life. Since watching the EMTs work on her while she was still strapped upside down in our car, my whole existence had been focused on getting her back. Miraculously, God had saved her life, and I was impatient to pick up where we left off and build a future together. But that assumed we would be building on a shared past. Suddenly the past was gone. And I had no idea when, if ever, Krickitt's memory would return.

Her neuropsychologist at Barrow, Dr. Kevin Obrien, explained to me in as encouraging a way as he could what Krickitt's diagnosis was, and what I had to look forward to from this point. The accident actually had caused two kinds of amnesia. The first, post-traumatic amnesia, was a temporary confusion about where she was and what was going on around her. Krickitt was already much less affected by this type of amnesia, and it would soon disappear completely.

The second type was retrograde amnesia, a permanent loss of short-term memory. We already knew her memory about people and events from the distant past had returned. She remembered her parents, brother, and sister-in-law. She remembered her old roommate Lisa Eberly. For better or worse, she remembered her old boyfriend Todd. But as far as anything that had happened within the previous year and a half, the tape had been erased. It was a complete blank. And in that year and a half we had met, dated, gotten engaged, married, had our honeymoon in Hawaii, and started our life together in Las Vegas. She didn't remember any of it; she didn't even remember anything about the wreck.

Nights at my in-laws', I lay awake thinking about what to do, afraid one minute, mad the next, and confused all the way around. *What would life be like from now on? What kind of person would Krickitt turn out to be? Would she always be different? Was the awesome, Spirit-filled young woman I married still in there, or was she gone for good? When would we know she had improved as much as she was going to?* It was all I thought about. I couldn't sleep, I couldn't relax, couldn't get rid of the stress. Though she still had a chance to recover part of her lost memory, the doctors knew there were some things she would never remember.

Would one of those things be me?

We settled into a daily routine with Krickitt's therapy at Barrow. I saw steady progress in her coordination, walking, speech, and reasoning. When she started walking on her own, she jerked her right foot forward, then dragged the left one on the floor behind her. Gradually the movement got smoother and more natural. Before long she could dress by herself, eat, and take care of all the basic necessities. She didn't seem to mind me being around, and talked to me like she talked to all the other familiar faces in the rehab center—cordial, even friendly, but without any depth or dimension. It was strictly a 2-D conversation.

Krickitt's physical therapist was Scott Madsen, an energetic trainer who had a special gift for encouraging his patients to do just a little more every day than they thought they could possibly do. He worked with Krickitt on the treadmill, with hand weights, and doing a range of exercises designed to help her get as much flexibility and strength back as possible.

After he had been working with her for a week or two, I had the strong impression that Krick was getting a little bored with the whole process. I thought they were going too easy on her. I was a coach, and I thought I saw a need for a fairly heavy dose of coaching along with the rehab. Krickitt wasn't putting enough into it. She needed to be pushed a little.

One day when the time seemed right I said, "Scott, you're going too easy on her. This patient is not your ordinary car-crash victim. She is an academic, All-American athlete who went to Cal State on a gymnastics scholarship. You need to push a little more."

Scott agreed to cheer Krickitt on to do more. I was encouraged, but Krickitt was unhappy with the new standards. She pouted and complained, and instead of her physical therapist, she insisted Scott had become her "physical terrorist," always wanting more, never satisfied.

Krickitt said Scott was making her walk on the treadmill for an hour at a time now, even though actually it was only a few minutes. I didn't think the change in her routine was all that drastic; besides, Scott wasn't about to deviate from what he thought was in his patient's interest, no matter what I said. Still, the physical therapy got more physical, and Krickitt got more unhappy.

Ever since she had started talking again, she had acted strangely childlike. This childishness hadn't gone away; in fact, it seemed to have become a permanent part of her personality. When she was dissatisfied in therapy or mad at me for something I'd done, she had mood swings and tantrums like a preschooler, and sudden outbursts of temper like the one she'd had the first day the doctor came in and woke her up. She had a little girl's lack of subtlety and propriety and had no fear of telling anybody exactly what she thought about them or their suggestions. It was a far cry from the polite, amiable, easy-going Krickitt of the past.

This, I learned, was common for someone with her injuries. The frontal lobe of her brain had been damaged, the part that controls personality, emotions, and decision-making. Her parietal lobe was also affected, which meant there likely would be permanent changes in her language and mathematical comprehension ability. Not only would her body be different from now on; her personality would be too. Again, no one knew how much she would improve before she got to her final recovery plateau.

As Krickitt's therapy continued, she kept getting stronger. That was encouraging, but what excited me even more was that she started having "flash memories" or "snapshot memories," mental pictures of something happening at a specific moment during the past year, but nothing that connected it with her life before or after. One morning some activity in the physical therapy room reminded her of working out on a stair-stepper; she couldn't remember anything on either side of it, but it was one more link with her—our—missing past. She remembered sitting outside at a table surrounded by lush tropical plants. That was our honeymoon, though I wasn't in her picture, at least not yet.

She also remembered something about church or the Bible, a kind of faith snapshot that stirred up memories of what she called "this Christianity thing." As scrambled as her thinking was, an awareness of God was one of the first things she had talked about when she came out of her coma. Her brother, Jamey, was sure she was still a believer, still had faith in God and understood Him at some level. I took a lot of comfort from what he said one afternoon after we'd been together with Krickitt most of the day.

"Krickitt's Christianity is in her core, Kim—it's part of her soul," he told me. "And her soul can't be affected by any injury because it's immortal. Her faith will always be there. It's there now. God has preserved her for some great purpose, and her faith is there to carry her through."

Advice like this from Jamey and other members of the family helped me keep myself pasted together. As surely as God had saved Krick for some great purpose, He also had surrounded me with loving, supportive people I could talk to. When you're a guy—and especially when you're a coach—it's like the world assumes you're supposed to suck it up and get on with life. But I absolutely could not have made it without my parents, my brothers, and Gus and Mary to share the burden. I would have flamed out if I'd tried to keep everything inside.

Besides depending on my family for support, I made a decision to become as much of an expert as I could on head injury rehabilitation. I wanted to do my homework so I could understand exactly what Krickitt was going through and what I could do to help her best. The doctors and therapists at Barrow were very patient in answering my questions and explaining all the details as well as they could in layman's terms. Knowledge is power; our greatest fear in life is fear of the unknown. I promised myself I would never let fear control my life or my marriage. There is no fear in love—God shows us that perfect love casts out fear.

The new year began with the now-familiar slow, steady progress, a little more improvement every week. Krickitt's mood swings were still wild and unpredictable, and she complained regularly about Scott, her "physical terrorist," and the way he kept pressuring her to excel. On the positive side, she was stronger and more independent. She was going on short walks with staff members in the neighborhood around Barrow. She loved these outings, especially when they included the shopping center nearby. A near-fatal brain injury had not affected her love of cruising the aisles at the discount stores looking for a good deal on shoes.

In fact, she lobbied to go shopping more often, though she couldn't leave the grounds of the clinic by herself. Every door in that area of the hospital had a keypad on the wall beside it. Krickitt and all the other patients wore security bracelets, and whenever Krick approached a doorway she had to stop until a staff member punched in a code. If anyone wearing a bracelet walked through the door without the code being punched first, an alarm went off.

One day as I was walking down the hall with Krickitt and a nurse, we all stopped short of the door so the nurse could key in the code. But before she could step forward, Krickitt punched it in herself. She'd learned it by watching the nurses. That meant they had to change the security code for the entire clinic. Nobody was really upset about it, though. In fact, I took it as one more encouraging sign of Krickitt's recovery. One more little hint of that old spark.

I looked for signs of the old Krickitt everywhere in everything. I was convinced that the way to bring her back was to help her tackle the rehab program with real fire and enthusiasm. I couldn't reach her as a husband, but I could as a coach. So I traded one identity for the other, coming to her PT sessions with Scott and pushing them both to pick up the pace. If he told her to do ten sit-ups, I wanted twenty; if he wanted her to walk four minutes on the treadmill, I wanted eight.

A week or two into the new year, Krickitt and I were playing whiffle ball. I tossed it to her underhanded, and she swung and missed time and again.

"Come on, Krick," I prodded, "I know you can nail it. Let's try again."

"I'm tired," she answered, in the pouty tones of a six-year-old.

"Let's do this a few more times."

"I don't want to."

"Please?" As I said it, I tossed her the ball again. Pressing her lips together she gave a mighty swing, connected with the whiffle ball, and hit a line drive that sailed over the volleyball net.

I was elated. "That's it, Krick! Way to go!"

"You're mean to me."

"Not mean," I answered back. "Just trying to help." For the thousandth time I looked hard for the shadow of the girl I had fallen so incredibly in love with. I knew she was in that slowly recovering body, aching to get out. She had to be.

The daily therapy sessions became a challenge for her. Not that they were difficult physically—she was doing an excellent job, and Scott and I cheered her on constantly. She was just bored and distracted. She was doing all this not because she wanted to or felt it was helping her, but because people kept making her. I got more out of her therapy sessions than she did. My rehabilitation from the wreck was watching her recover.

It was two steps forward and one step back. A session would be going along well and she'd stop all of a sudden and say, "I'm tired. I want to go sit down."

"Hey, Krick, let's just do a few more reps of this."

"I don't want to! Stop bossing me around! You don't play fair!"

She'd be working on movement and coordination in the swimming pool, then quit doing the exercises and announce simply, "I'm going to the hot tub."

If it had been up to me at that point, she never would have come near a hot tub. I was heavily into tough-love mode. Her parents and the staff at Barrow did what they could to balance out her demands with what they knew she needed. But Krickitt was shameless when it came to pulling people's strings.

One of Krickitt's few true pleasures was food, and her favorite snack was yogurt. Knowing this helped us get her to do things she didn't want to do, because we usually could bribe her with a cup of frozen yogurt. However, she was not above putting a big guilt trip on anyone she thought might cave in and give her a treat when she actually hadn't earned it. (Once in a great while she was even successful.)

No matter what I did, I couldn't seem to build more than a casual friendship with her. When I tried to play volleyball, she quit playing. When I went jogging with her, her comments and complaints got steadily more personal and cutting. I never knew what to expect from one day to the next. One minute she'd be friendly and smiling, then I'd do something wrong, and in a heartbeat she'd look at me and bark, "Leave me alone! I don't even know who you are!"

It was a game of psychological ping-pong. One afternoon, still stinging after some sharp rebuke earlier in the day, I walked into the PT room and found Krickitt lying on her stomach on the carpet, head up, chin resting in the palms of her hands, feet slowly paddling up and down. So quiet and thoughtful.

"What you thinking about, Krick?"

She turned her face toward me, still resting her chin on her hands, then turned back. She paused and slowly shook her head.

"Life is so confusing," she said slowly. Then, looking back over at me, "Are we really married?"

"We're really married, Krickitt. I love you."

Another slow shake of the head. Then only silence.

Was this the new reality? Maybe I was waiting for some kind of recovery or reconnection that never was going to happen. As I walked out of the room I thought, *Is this it? Maybe this is the best it's ever going to be.* For the first time I consciously let myself believe she might not ever be the same person. Very possibly, the woman I married no longer existed. Some of the literature the hospital gave us about head injuries explained that her recovery could stop suddenly at any point.

In a way it was harder to deal with than death. If Krickitt had died in the wreck, there would have been a clear ending to our life together. As horrible as it would have been, I could have dealt with it, I thought, because I understood what death was. What I had instead was life in some hazy emotional, spiritual, and relational netherworld where my wife was still here, but at the same time she wasn't.

On one hand I wondered how our lives would have been different if we had gone along the way we'd started. I longed for all those years we now would never have. But on the other, we had a chance to build a new future together. She was still with me. She still could have a life. I had to accept the fact that it would be different from the life I had been looking forward to. But God must have preserved her like this for some great purpose he could see that I couldn't.

After a month at Barrow, the doctors started telling us Krickitt could soon be released to live with her parents and continue therapy as an outpatient. Krickitt was delighted at the thought, both because she would be with her family, and because she would spend less time around her physical terrorist and her demanding husband/father/coach figure—me.

On January 13, 1994, almost seven weeks after the accident, Krickitt moved into her parents' house in Phoenix. She seemed to like having familiar things around: her college yearbooks, photo albums, scrapbooks, furniture she'd grown up with, and mementos from her childhood. Her mom showed her our wedding pictures. They were only proofs. The photographer had sent them to Gus and Mary while we were getting settled in Las Vegas, and we were going to pick out the ones we wanted for our keepsake album over Thanksgiving.

I sat beside Krickitt on the couch as she flipped through them. It had been quite a show—Krick in her exquisite wedding gown, me in white tie and tails, the front of the church lit entirely by candles. We all hoped seeing the pictures would spark some more of those flash memories and help her pick up a thread that would lead back to more detailed memories of our marriage. She recognized the bride in the pictures as herself, but that was as far as it went. There was still no emotional connection.

The ping-pong game continued. One day I'd be riding high because Krickitt had walked farther than ever before on the treadmill, or read something she couldn't read the day before, or had another flash memory. The next I was depressed and miserable because she had lashed out at me again for pushing her in therapy, or one more memory jogger—a picture, a name, a letter—had failed to bring back anything about our life together.

I hadn't worked in two months, but college athletics were the last thing on my mind. All I thought about day and night was Krickitt and what I could do to help her get better. I was still getting no pressure from the administration at Highlands, and the assistant coaches were gearing up for spring training without me there. My parents and in-laws, however, were convinced that the best thing I could do at this point was to get back to our home in Las Vegas, get back to coaching baseball, and make it a priority to restore some sort of normalcy to life. At first I was totally against leaving Krickitt. But the more they talked, the more I agreed it was the right thing to do.

I called Gilbert Sanchez at Highlands and told him I was ready to come back.

"We're anxious to have you," he said, "but we don't want you back until you're ready. Take your time."

"I've taken my time," I answered, "and we're all ready to start getting things back to normal. I want the Highlands Cowboys off to a good start, and I want to be a part of it."

That was all true. What was also true was that I needed to be around something I could understand and predict and have some control over. By God's grace I had made it this far with Krickitt, but I sensed it was time to trust him even more. He would work His perfect will with my wife whether I was in Phoenix or Las Vegas. She had her parents—people she remembered and loved—to take care of her. It was time for me to get home and prepare a place for her there.

My first official day back on campus would be February 1, but I made one quick trip before that in preparation for my return. While I was there, I kept a fairly low profile, knowing I'd be gone again soon before coming home for good. I went into the locker room at Highlands to change the bandages on my back. There I saw a home-made handbill about a fund drive for Coach Carpenter and his wife. Somebody at school had organized an appeal to help us pay our expenses. This was a community where people had precious little to give, yet they were doing this for us. I didn't let anyone know I was onto their surprise. Besides, I didn't have any idea exactly what they were going to do.

I went back to Phoenix, said good-bye to Krickitt and her parents, and returned to our apartment in Las Vegas. I opened the door to find it freshly cleaned, and a hot dinner in the oven. At practice the next day the players couldn't have been nicer or more supportive. Even though I had left them without a head coach for more than two months, all they cared about was me and Krickitt and us getting better. It was an awesome testament to the value of godly friends.

After practice, a couple of the players came over to me and said, "Coach Carpenter, there are some people over here who'd like to talk to you." I followed them around the corner, and there was a group of friends and coworkers from Highlands standing there waiting for me.

One of them stepped forward. "We want you to have this," she said. She handed me a huge pickle jar full of money. For weeks they had sponsored bake sales and raffles and solicited donations to raise money so I could fly back to Phoenix every week to be with Krickitt. There were checks in that jar from people I knew for a fact were broke, and when they weren't broke, they still didn't have much of anything. There were also monetary gifts from judges and other prominent people in town. Altogether it was enough for ten round-trip tickets between Albuquerque and Phoenix.

I set up an ambitious plan for spending time with Krickitt every week, even though she was five hundred miles from my baseball team. Early Monday morning I drove two hours from our apartment in Las Vegas, New Mexico, to the airport in Albuquerque, caught a plane for Phoenix, and stayed with Krick through Wednesday night. Thursday I caught a 5:30 A.M. return flight to Albuquerque, drove two hours back to the campus at Highlands in Las Vegas, and got to the field in time for Thursday workouts with the team for our games that weekend. When there were away games, I drove the bus, which meant some Sunday nights I didn't get back to our apartment until well after midnight. Monday morning I started all over again.

Clearly this wasn't going to work long-term. I wasn't sleeping much anyway on account of all the stress and my back trouble, and this totally unrealistic schedule gave me even less time to rest. On top of it all, the calls from bill collectors were starting to get out of hand. Krickitt's medical expenses alone were already more than $150,000. Then there were my medical bills, Krickitt's continuing rehab, and other incidentals which pushed the total debt to a hair over $200,000. By now we knew that it was not going to be smooth sailing with our insurance company. We got in touch with them early on, but they were not going to settle for what we needed to satisfy the collection agencies any time soon. That meant we were facing the prospect of a lawsuit just to get our insurance carrier to pay the money we thought our premiums already entitled us to. That, in turn, meant hiring lawyers and going even further into debt with the hope they could fix everything.

And as much as I looked forward to my visits with Krickitt, her attitude toward me got worse instead of better. Monday afternoons I'd go straight from the airport to Barrow to help her with her therapy. Sometimes she would greet me in a friendly way when I came in, and sometimes she'd just grunt something in my direction and go on with whatever she was doing.

Encouraging her was like poking at a time bomb. In my heart I wanted her to improve so much, and I knew as a coach you have to push people to achieve their potential—they're not always going to see how far they can go as well as a coach can. I pushed her because I thought it was my duty to push her. One little nudge of encouragement might not get any reaction from her, but the next one could set off a shower of enraged screaming.

"Quit telling me what to do! Leave me alone!" she said day after day, eyes shooting darts at me, hair flying.

"I'm only trying to help you get better. You want to get better, right?"

"LEAVE ME ALONE! I HATE YOU!! WHY DON'T YOU GO BACK TO LAS VEGAS OR WHEREVER IT IS YOU CAME FROM!?"

"Because I love you."

Her face frozen in a bitter stare, she turned away without another word, day after day, week after week. And every week on the Thursday red-eye back to Albuquerque, I looked down at the desert as the sun came up ahead of me. The faint glow of the sunrise always reminded me of the glow that had filled the church that night the September before when I watched the woman of my dreams—the woman God had saved for me alone—walk down the aisle bathed in candlelight. There, holding my hand in front of our families and everyone we loved, she looked steadily into my eyes and said in a clear, confident voice everyone in the church could hear:

"Finally today is here, the day that I give you my hand in marriage. I'm honored to be your wife."

"I'm all yours, Kimmer. And I love you."

Chapter 6

MY LIFETIME BUDDY

I always loved baseball. My dad coached some in Farmington when I was growing up, and I was on top of the world when I got my first coaching job with the Highlands Cowboys at Highlands University in Las Vegas, New Mexico. Some time around the start of the school year in the fall of 1992, I was flipping through catalogs from sports uniform companies and found some cool-looking jackets I thought our assistant coaches and managers would look good in.

I called the 800 number, and after a couple of rings a voice came on the line: "Good morning, and thanks for calling Jammin'. This is Krickitt." It wasn't the usual 800-number monotone. This was a voice with some real vitality and interest to it. When she said, "Good morning," it sounded like she meant it.

"Hi, Krickitt," I answered, "my name is Coach Carpenter and I'm from New Mexico Highlands University. I'm calling about the baseball coaches' jackets in your catalog."

It was a really mundane conversation. Even so, as we talked prices, colors, and item numbers, I got more and more interested in this telephone salesperson named Krickitt. She sounded so friendly and helpful—a real ray of sunshine in an otherwise ordinary day.

She answered my questions, and we hung up. But I couldn't stop thinking about her. There was something different and special about the voice and the person that I really couldn't explain. She seemed genuinely interested in helping me. It wasn't just a job, it was more like a mission; like she had decided to be the friendliest, most helpful person her customers talked to every day.

A few days later I decided to call again. "Good morning, and thanks for calling Jammin'. This is Keri." Keri was fine, but hearing her made me face the fact that I was calling for something besides buying a coach's jacket.

"Keri, this is Coach Carpenter at New Mexico Highlands University. I'm following up on an order with Krickitt."

"Just a minute." My pulse picked up.

"Hi, this is Krickitt. What can I do for you today?"

"Hi, Krickitt. Coach Carpenter with the Highlands Cowboys. I called about a jacket the other day."

"Sure, Coach. Let me just get that in front of me."

What was it about this Krickitt person that made my heart rate go up a couple of notches? She was a sales rep, for Pete's sake, sitting there at an order desk in California taking orders for athletic jackets and gym bags. I asked her for some color samples and we hung up.

The samples came in the mail in a few days. Laying them out on a table, I wondered if she had picked them out herself. Had she held them in her hands? *Wait a minute.* I was thinking like a high school kid with a secret crush! What in the world had gotten into me?

Whatever it was, I was unusually eager to talk to a telephone sales rep when I called again to order a purple and gray jacket for the

Highlands Cowboys. "Good morning, and thanks for calling Jammin'. This is Krickitt."

"Hi, Krickitt, it's Coach Carpenter. I . . ."

"Coach Carpenter!" She interrupted with a sense of excitement that surprised me, considering I was about to order exactly one jacket. "It's great to hear from you again."

Was she just glad for an order, or glad to hear from me? Was I kidding myself, or did I sense more than a professional friendliness in the sound of her voice?

I ordered the jacket. After it came, I ordered another one in a different style. It looked so good, every coach and manager on the team wanted one, so I ordered some more. Four or five months had passed since our first conversation, and by now, every time Krickitt and I talked, we spent a lot more time visiting than we did on business. Then one day at the end of a call, she mentioned she would probably be off on the day I was going to call to check on an order. So she gave me her number at home. No doubt her bosses were happy about that, because we had gotten to where we tied up the 800 number fairly seriously.

I started calling her at her apartment, and before long we dropped any pretense of talking about sports uniforms and spent the time talking about ourselves and each other. The conversations stretched to an hour and beyond. (We also wrote letters quite frequently.) No matter how long we talked, it seemed neither of us could get enough. My phone bill shot up from almost nothing to $500 a month. But she was worth it.

Krickitt was a nickname for Krisxan (pronounced "Kris-Ann"), a name that reflected her Greek ancestry. She got it when she was two from an aunt who swore she could never sit still and hopped around all the time like a cricket. Her dad had once coached high school wrestling, basketball, and baseball. Her mother coached gymnastics, which Krickitt loved from the time she was old enough to walk on a balance beam. In fact, Krick could do a back handspring before she could print her name.

I thought I loved sports, but she lived sports. She'd practiced every day after school and five hours a day in the summers practically since she was in kindergarten, starting out in a gym her mother had owned. When she was sixteen, she tore the rotator cuff in her right shoulder, but didn't have surgery because her coaches told her an operation would probably kill her chances for a scholarship. So she kept at it, excelling in floor exercises and the balance beam, working through the pain in her shoulder every day.

Sure enough, she had her pick of schools and went to California State University at Fullerton on a full-ride gymnastics scholarship. She was a two-time academic All-American there before giving up competition after she tore her anterior cruciate ligament—in gymnasts' terms, "blew out her knee"—when she was a senior. (Seniors, she said, were grandmas on the team anyway.)

So sports were an important part of life for both of us. We also learned we were both Christians and had discovered Christ at the same age, but from that point our spiritual journeys had gone in different directions.

I first found out about Jesus from a girl who was baby-sitting at a friend's house. I thought learning that Christ died for me and that my sins were forgiven was the most awesome news I'd ever heard in all my fourteen years. I went home on fire for the Lord and couldn't wait to talk to my parents about it. But when I got to the house and started telling them what I felt, it didn't click with them at all. They were nominal churchgoers, but I don't think they'd ever felt what I was feeling at that moment. We had never gone to mass regularly, and religion was simply not something we ever went into in depth. I had felt Christ pierce my heart, but in an hour it was like it had never happened. Still, the seed was planted, and in time I came fully and completely to accept Jesus as Lord.

Krickitt found Jesus in her brother's room. One day she came across a little booklet he had titled *The Four Spiritual Laws* and started leafing through it. The message filled her with excitement and curiosity. No one knew she prayed to receive Christ on that day. She didn't even totally know, at the time, what she had done for eternity. She never confirmed this decision with anyone and never got involved in church programs. It wasn't until college that she went to the Evangelical Free Church in Fullerton (which she and her friends called Eve Free) and felt her spiritual life transformed by the pastor there, Charles Swindoll, and also by the college pastor, Steve McCracken.

In the summer of 1991, Steve led a mission trip to Hungary. Krickitt had just wrecked her knee and suddenly, after years of grueling workout schedules, had time on her hands because she couldn't work out with the team. When the Hungary trip came up, she saw it as a God-given opportunity to pour all the time and energy she had always put into gymnastics into something else. She and her friend (and later roommate) Megan Almquist went along, and spent nine weeks sharing their testimonies with Christians and seekers starved for the gospel after generations of oppression.

I thought I was reasonably close to the Lord, but Krickitt Pappas put me to shame. Her faith was interwoven with every part of her life. She wasn't a Sunday Christian; she was an every-minute-of-every-day Christian.

Our phone conversations got increasingly longer and more involved. I started calling her "Slick Krick, my phone friend chick." We wrote back and forth, and she started signing her notes that way. The letters were like the phone calls—they were short cards at first but got longer and longer until Slick Krick was writing me ten pages at a time.

I guess it was inevitable that the idea of exchanging pictures would come up, and early in the spring of 1993 we decided to give it a whirl. I sent her a Highlands Cowboys media guide with my picture as head coach in it. Then I waited impatiently for a snapshot that would put a face with this perky voice I liked so much and the personality behind it. I told myself I was interested strictly in her heart and her spirit; but at the same time, I figured it couldn't hurt if she happened to be a babe.

I wasn't disappointed. When the odd-sized envelope came in the mail a few days later, I ripped it open, held my breath, and cast my eyes upon a beautiful woman with dark hair, sparkling blue eyes, and a fantastic smile. She was gorgeous.

The only strange thing was that there had obviously been another person in the picture, but whoever it was had been cut out. Around Krickitt's shoulder I thought I could see an arm that belonged to the missing face. Was it her boyfriend? Another "special friend" like me? Curiosity was eating me up. "Take it easy," I said softly out loud. "You're getting way ahead of yourself."

I couldn't wait to call her that night to see if she'd gotten my picture too. "Got it!" she answered. I waited. "And you know, I thought, 'This guy is even cute.'" We both laughed. I had been afraid the picture thing would be tense, but it was like talking to a lifelong friend.

"I noticed you edited your picture for me."

"Yeah." Again I waited, expectant. "I cut my girlfriends out because they are gorgeous!" We both laughed as before. Her voice was like music, and it was fast becoming my favorite song.

For all the fun we had, she wasted no time getting to the spiritual part of our relationship. In the first letter she sent after we swapped pictures (ten solid pages), she wrote:

"You said I can ask you anything, so I must be honest, Kimmer. You know that I am a Christian. Being a Christian is having an ongoing intimate relationship with Jesus Christ. I guess what I have been wondering this whole time is if you were a Christian too—if you had made the decision to ask Christ into your life to pay the penalty of your sin, and give you eternal life like he has promised if we ask."

Her faith was her life, and no matter how cute I looked in my baseball uniform (she thought it made me look like a little boy), she had to have a peace about my spiritual side before she could have any sort of relationship. I think she was a little nervous about bringing it up, but it just made me like her all the more.

The next step would be a big one, and we both knew it. We'd actually started talking about meeting in person in February. We were talking five-plus hours a week, and at that rate a plane ticket seemed more like a bargain every day. I asked her if she'd like to come to Las Vegas and see the Cowboys play. She said she didn't know. She'd have to think and pray about it.

After we'd talked about it several times, she leveled with me in another letter (thirteen pages!) about her concerns:

"It would be so fun to meet my sweet friend Coach Carpenter and watch your team play. I guess, to be honest, I don't want you to feel like you have any expectations of me, nor I have expectations of you. And I'm sure you'll think I'm silly for saying that, but also, I know you are a very well-respected 'feller' there, and I wouldn't want to be one ever to jeopardize your reputation that you have there, even though we are just buddies. I don't want them to think wrong of you. Does that make sense? But, on the other hand, it would be really fun to meet my phone pal."

It took us two solid months to work through it, but as the baseball season got underway, she made the decision to let me fly her to New Mexico so we could meet face-to-face. "I've got a real peace about it," she told me in our last phone call before the trip. I drove the two hours to Albuquerque to pick her up. Of course, I spotted her the second she walked through the jetway. I felt we had so much in common and had such a wonderful friendship already. Now that I saw her I could hardly believe how beautiful she was.

"Well here I am!" she announced. After so many hours on the phone, I had a living, breathing person to put with that wonderful voice. With no phone bill to worry about, we literally talked all weekend. I had gotten a hotel room so Krickitt could stay either there or at my apartment, whichever made her more comfortable, and I would stay at the other place.

But at the end of the evening, we decided to talk awhile before going our separate ways. We talked about everything: our childhoods, our families, our jobs, our love of sports, the fact that both our dads had been baseball coaches, our friends, and our incredible long-distance relationship.

Most of all we talked about our faith. She was so much more mature as a Christian than I was, but she didn't beat me over the head with her superior understanding. She encouraged me to get to know

God better and to give myself completely to him. She was so confident and assured—her example was more inspiring than any sermon I'd ever heard.

Eventually we both stopped to catch our breath at the same time. In the silence, Krickitt glanced out the window, then pointed with astonishment written on her face. It was broad daylight. We'd talked all night without missing a beat.

The Cowboys lost the first game of the home stand by one run. Then they lost the second game by one run. Bummer. As Krickitt and I began our second evening together, I got even more depressed talking about my mother, who was going through a serious illness. Somehow Krickitt drew me out in a way no one ever had before. It wasn't like I was complaining. It was that she understood me and sympathized with me in a way I'd never felt, and I knew she wanted to know about my fears and challenges. I wanted to know the same about her.

A few minutes into our conversation she pulled out a present. "For you," she said, obviously delighted at taking me completely by surprise. I opened the box, and inside was a beautiful new Bible with my name stamped on it in gold. I didn't know what to say. By the time I could mumble something like "Thank you," she was already turning to the Book of Job.

"Life isn't fair; it's life," she said softly, confidently. "God seems absent in everybody's life some time or another. But he's always there, always refining your faith, always bringing you closer to him, even when your mother's sick and your baseball team stinks."

She started to read: "In the land of Uz there lived a man whose name was Job. This man was blameless and upright. . . ." After awhile she stopped, and we talked about Job's terrible trials. *Why would God let such awful things happen to such a good man? And in the middle of it all, why didn't Job throw in the towel and renounce his faith?*

She read, I read, and we talked as the hours passed. When we got to the end of the story, Job's faith was richly rewarded. And sometime in the small hours of the morning we both fell asleep on the couch. Again, she never went to her hotel. The next day Krickitt flew back to California. (And I fell asleep coaching third base.) Dropping her at the airport at the beginning of the weekend, her roommate Lisa had told her she felt like she was somehow saying good-bye to her for good. When she picked her up, she saw stars in her eyes. Her feminine intuition told her it was only a matter of time before her roommate would be flying the coop.

I'm sure we both had friends who whispered about our "spending the weekend" together. It was exhilarating and exciting and completely awesome. And yet all weekend I never even kissed her. Never even tried to.

A couple of days after she left, I got a thank-you card from her. It was so beautiful it made me miss her more than ever. Besides, she wrote with such conviction—and absolutely nailed my own feelings about the situation. Girls seem to have a knack for that.

Believe it or not, she got all of this on a single card and had room left over for a big picture of Snoopy:

> Kimmo—
> I think back over this weekend and it was filled with so much laughter and tears—it was truly wonderful. I would never have imagined that we would be so compatible together. I enjoyed getting to know you this weekend. I feel so special to have seen who the real Kim Carpenter is. You have a heart that is so beautiful to me. Your lovingkindness, gentleness, humility, craziness, and

uniqueness completely blew me away. The way you have opened up to me and trusted me with who you are and what you have been through means so much to me.

I, too, am blown away by some of the things we have talked about. I prayed so much for our weekend together, that we would enjoy one another's company and have quality conversations. Well, I guess He answered that one, huh?!! I have many questions and wonders with us. I am curious to know what is going to happen. I am ready to go with this relationship and see where it is going to go. It's not in our hands, Kimmer. I think we can go forward and go towards first base. I'm scared, but risk is part of love. I feel that the Lord is either going to continue to open the doors for us, or He will shut them. I'm placing this in His hands and trusting Him. Thank you for treating me so kind and making me feel so special and adored.

Well, Kim Carpenter, I adore & cherish you.
All my love,
Krickitt
Philippians 4:6-9 Read and dwell on this.

We talked every day that following week. The next weekend I had some time off, and Krickitt agreed to come back for another visit. We went hiking one day and four-wheeling the next, driving up into the mountains where there was still snow on the ground even in April.

A couple of weeks later, I had a recruiting trip to San Diego and couldn't resist dovetailing it with a visit to Krickitt in Anaheim. I met her parents, her brother and sister-in-law, and some of her friends. They were all so kind and welcoming—her father, Gus, and I hit it off right away. Anybody who ever coached baseball has to be a pretty good guy. We met for pizza in Newport Beach, and I saw things there that you don't see much of in Las Vegas, New Mexico: Mercedes-Benzes with little wipers on the headlights, for instance, and commuter lanes on the freeway limited to cars with additional passengers. I hated to see all that empty pavement going to waste. So in the interest of improved traffic flow on the L.A. freeway, I propped a duffel bag up in the front seat beside me and put a hat on it.

I went to church with Krickitt at Eve Free—First Evangelical Free Church of Fullerton. Charles Swindoll was an incredible preacher whose passion for the Holy Spirit was powerful and compelling. Krickitt's world was the world of Christ. The more I understood about her faith, the more I understood about her. And vice versa.

Late in May I took some vacation days and returned to California. We had come to another crossroads in our relationship. Our feelings for each other were obviously deep and sincere. Were we in love? Was it time to think about marriage? I loved her so much, but I wanted to love her for all the right reasons and with all the right intentions.

We drove to Chevy's Mexican Restaurant and then went walking on the beach at Del Mar. We weren't our usual gabby selves; instead we talked sparingly, like each of us knew what the other one was going to say and that every word was special and important.

It was decision time; what should we do? I couldn't imagine life from this point forward without Krickitt. But we had jobs and families hundreds of miles apart. We'd only met each other in person eight weeks earlier. Could we already be so sure we were prepared to spend the rest of our lives together?

Even this early in the year, the southern California days were starting to get hot, but the night air was cool and fresh as we walked along together by the surf. We cast long, soft shadows in the glow of distant streetlights—shadows that stretched all the way to the water, then merged into one at the edge of the darkness.

There were times that night when I thought we would have to end our relationship. It couldn't stay like it was; it could only go forward or back. Should we part now before we got in too deep emotionally, or was it already too late for that? Should one of us move? Should Krickitt quit her job? Should I quit mine? We had to decide, even though it seemed for the longest time that all we'd be able to do that night was walk along the beach holding hands and crying. Eventually marriage worked its way into the conversation, not in an excited or emotional way, but in a strangely calm way, as though it were one logical possible outcome of a situation we wanted to see through to the finish. We agreed it was an option, and Krickitt told me I would have to ask her father for her hand in marriage.

Mr. and Mrs. Pappas were in Omaha, Nebraska, for the College Baseball World Series (a good sign!). I got back home to Las Vegas and called them at their hotel.

Gus and I exchanged a few pleasantries and talked about the series. Finally, I took a deep breath and said, "I want to marry your daughter and she says I have to ask you."

"Oh, you do?"

"Yes, sir."

"We'd be honored to have you as our son-in-law."

Thinking about the conversation turned out to be a lot more stressful than the conversation itself.

I was determined to be creative when I proposed to Krickitt. Back in California, I bought a diamond ring, then called Krick's roommates, Megan and Lisa, to help me set the stage for my next visit. Their apartment had a security gate, and I wanted one of her roomies to answer the buzzer so I could surprise Krickitt. They were happy to play along, and got me inside the apartment complex. I showed up outside Krickitt's apartment in a suit and tie. (This was in spite of the fact that it was a sweltering June day and coaches have a genetic aversion to dress clothes even when it's cool.) Then I started yelling Krickitt's name.

In a minute she came out onto her balcony, my Juliet in shorts and Nikes. I was holding flowers, a teddy bear with balloons tied to it, and a ring box.

The sight struck her speechless, but only for an instant. "What are you doing here?" she hollered down.

"Well . . . Will ya?" I shouted back.

She disappeared from the balcony and, in a second, came flying down the stairs.

"Will I what?" The wind played in her hair. Her skin was luminescent in the summer sun. Her eyes shimmered like diamonds.

I got down on one knee, just like in the movies.

"Will you be my lifetime buddy? Krisxan, will you marry me?"

Hardly a pause at all. Just enough time to take a breath.

"Yes, I will."

The next thing we said was, "Now what do we do!?"

I'd thought we would get married by the following spring. "I don't think I can wait a year," Krickitt finally admitted. *Fine with me!* Christmas? Still too far off for her. And so we set September 18, barely three months off, as the big day. By that time we would have known each other almost exactly a year, half by phone and half in person.

I went back to Las Vegas to get our apartment ready, and Krickitt went to work picking out a wedding dress, china, and all the other traditional wedding goodies. She started making arrangements long distance from Anaheim for a ceremony at Scottsdale Bible Church in suburban Phoenix, where her brother, Jamey, had been married.

We wrote our own wedding vows. And so it was that on the evening of September 18, a perfect late-summer desert night, I stood at the altar with more than a hundred friends, family, and guests looking on, held Krickitt's hand in mine, and said:

"Krisxan, I've grown to love you very much. I thank you for loving me in the beautiful ways that you have, and I will always, always cherish this beautiful moment. I promise to love and respect you fully. I promise to provide for and protect you through times of challenge and need. I promise to be faithful, honest, and open; to devote myself to your every need and desire. Most of all, I promise to be the man you so fell in love with. And thank you, Jesus, for the blessing you have provided me in Krisxan. I love you."

Krickitt's response filled me to overflowing with thanksgiving and love:

"Kimmer, I love you. Finally today is here, the day that I give you my hand in marriage. I promise to be faithful to you, to love you in good times and bad, and to be equally ready to listen to you when you need to share. I promise to be open, and honest, and trustworthy, and I promise to support you each day. I'm honored to be your wife. I'm all yours, Kimmer. And I love you."

We made a vow.

The pastor asked Mike Kloeppel, my best man, for the ring. Mike reached under his coat, but instead of pulling out the ring, he pulled out . . . a baseball glove (formal black, of course). I couldn't let the wedding go by without at least one moment that was guaranteed unique. Mike handed me the glove; I put it on and signaled Krickitt's dad who was sitting in the front row. With a big grin he tossed a baseball up to me. I caught it, handed Mike back the glove, and then turned the baseball over until I found a square piece of white tape. I peeled it off and there underneath, nestled in a hole I'd routed out of the ball, was Krickitt's wedding ring. A love of sports had brought us together in the first place, so I thought it was only appropriate to mark our common interest in an unforgettable way—one that also symbolized Gus giving his daughter to me.

I took the new Mrs. Kim Carpenter to Maui for our honeymoon, and after that we settled in Las Vegas just as the new school year was getting under way. I started working with my team, and Krickitt launched into her new life with the same enthusiasm, spirit, and faith that had made her such a success in telephone sales. I was in my same town, at my same job, while Krick had been willing to start all over in a brand new environment. In no time she had become the team statistician, informal snack bar overseer, and all-around utility player wherever she saw a need.

She also took a position as an exercise technician in Northeastern Regional Hospital's Center for Health and Fitness on the campus of New Mexico Highlands University, a community fitness center where she designed exercise programs to help people reach their individual fitness goals. Her friendliness and gymnastics experience made her an instant hit.

Thanksgiving seemed like a perfect time to make our first visit to Krickitt's parents in Phoenix as Mr. and Mrs. Carpenter. Of course, she was excited about seeing her parents again, and I was looking forward to it too. They weren't just in-laws; they were fast becoming my good friends as well.

A few days before the Thanksgiving weekend, we started making plans for the trip. It was a long drive—more than five hundred miles—but it was all interstate with only one big city, Albuquerque, between us and the family Thanksgiving turkey.

Tuesday, the night before we left, we had a quiet dinner and then sat snuggling on the couch in front of the TV.

I had my arm around Krickitt, and she leaned her head on my chest. Out of the blue she looked up at me and asked, "Are you happy, Kimmer?"

The urge to kiss her was irresistible. Then I said, "I can't imagine how I could be any happier." And kissed her again.

Chapter 7

KRICKITT'S DIARY 2—
"Please guide my heart"

1/20/93

1 Corinthians 11:3 *"I want you to understand that Christ is the head of every man, and the man is the head of a woman, and God is the head of Christ."*

In thinking of my husband ruling over me, it really doesn't make me scared, because I know ruling above him is Christ. Knowing that *"you belong to Christ; and Christ belongs to God"* (1 Cor. 3:23) gives me a lot of security. It definitely is imp. to know that my husband will, prayerfully, be walking with God. How much easier it will be to submit to him, knowing that he is submitting to Christ.

—KP

1/28/93

Dear Jesus,

Well, today was a good day—very busy as usual.
I can't believe how fast one day can go. I enjoy it
though. Work is fun. I have to be honest, I think
Coach Carpenter sounds so sweet. I pray for his sal-
vation, I pray that I can be a good witness for him.
Help me be above reproach, Lord.

    —Love, KP

2/2/93

Lord Jesus,

God above all names, beautiful Savior, glorious
Lord, Emanuel, God is with me and I thank you for
that so, so much. I come to you, thanking you for
what great and awesome fellowship that I have. I
thank you for changing me and truly making me
able to spend time with friends. Lord, I pray for
Coach Carpenter. I don't know why he is in my
heart. Please open up his heart towards you.

    —KP

2/6/93

Lord,

I don't know why Coach Carpenter is on my mind, someone who I don't really know, but he seems as though he has a lot going for him. He seems different, at least his values and stuff. I pray for him. Lord, if he doesn't know you, I pray that he would come to see that he needs you in his life.

If it's your will for me to meet him, I pray I would. I enjoy his company. That would be great if he knew you, but I doubt it. I pray for our future conversations, that you would come up, so he knew where I stood, whether I talked to him at work or home. He's so nice. I know, Lord, that you have me in this life for a reason. Let me be a witness for you and a woman above reproach. I want to be seen as a quality person.

Lord, I know you know who I am going to marry, and I am sure that you will continue to pre-pare him for me. Please help me to develop into the gal you desire. I love you Lord.

—Krickitt

2/7/93

Lord,

I love you and I want you to be involved in every part of my life. Please show me those areas that I have not given over to you. I give my love life over to you. Even Coach Carpenter & our friendship. I pray for him, I pray we can continue to get to know one another. I pray for his team. Please provide a new pitching coach for them, if it's your will. Allow him to see he needs you. I don't know why I have this desire for his salvation. Is it selfish reasons? I pray not. It would be wonderful to have _you_ to talk to him of course. If I am to meet him, I pray I will. If not, then I pray our friendship could continue. He seems like a quality guy. I pray for some fun guy fellowship. I pray for purity in my mind. Sometimes I get so overwhelmed. Please forgive me for talking such girl talk these past few days. Purify my heart, make me clean & pure as snow. Thanks for your wonderful Holy Spirit and your faithfulness in my life. Please help me to be a woman of integrity & above reproach. Guard my heart & mind in Christ Jesus.

I pray for my husband—continue to prepare us for one another. I pray for his walk. Continue to strengthen & mature him in all aspects—please do the same for me. May I be a jewel to him & he to me. How I get excited about that day and trust you completely.

I pray for Jammin'. I really like it there & feel a sense of purpose & worth in all of their lives. Please Holy Spirit, continue to work through my life & convict their hearts that they need you. Open doors so I can share. Holy Spirit, help me to be bold & stand firm. Lord, please guide me, give me direction & wisdom. Show me what you want. Sometimes I think even about being a coach's wife. I love sports— I know you are showing me my interest, but I am so interested to see how you open and shut doors for my next move. Help me not to put qualifications that are not realistic on people—especially boys I meet.

—Love, Krickitt

2/11/93
I pray for Kimmer. I don't know why I have a burden for him & his family & a desire to know

him & share with him, but continue to open his heart if he doesn't know you.

2/16/93

1 Corinthians 16:14 "Let all that you do be done in love."

When I think of letting all I do be done in love, it really challenges me to look at my motives. There are so many times that my heart isn't right, and I do things out of obligation. But ultimately I should be doing things out of my love for the Lord, and allow his love really to flow out of me. Please allow your Spirit to continue to work in me and fill me with your love.

Please guide my steps and my heart. And once again, I pray for Coach Carpenter. I pray for a continued opening up of his mind and heart to you, I pray for an openness to hear your Word. Surround him with godly people. I pray for his mom and her salvation. Draw her near to you. I trust you, Lord, that if Kimmer is supposed to come out here, he will. Please be in control of my actions today. Holy Spirit, I _need_ you.

—KP

2/24/93

Lord Jesus,

It was nice to talk to Kimmer today. What a well-respected & fascinating person. I am enjoying getting to know him, and it was so sweet to hear that he believes in God & he wants to give glory to the Lord. That's the side of him I want to see. Please allow more conversations in the future to be based around you & the work you are doing. I pray for him; I pray that his relationship with you would become personal. Please be with Kimmer this weekend. I pray that you would begin revealing yourself to him. Allow him to see that he needs you. May I be a good example of godliness in his life. May he be open to you. May our friendship grow in the direction you have planned for it. May you keep me walking upright. I love you, Lord.

—Krisxan

2/26/93

Lord,

You are beautiful. Your face is all I see. I need you in the morning and 24 hrs. a day. I thank you for your constant guidance & love toward me. I

*thank you for my job & the fact that I enjoy it. Use
me to be a witness to those whom I work with. May
my sales glorify you. Lord, may you help me this
day to have peace & joy & patience. May I be your
witness & tool. May you be with Kimmer. I don't
know why he has been placed on my heart. But,
help me be obedient to pray for him. I love you,
Lord Jesus.*
  —KP

3/3/93
Dear Lord,
  *You have richly supplied my needs in many
ways. I cast my cares upon you, because you care
for me. Take today, make it be yours. May your
Holy Spirit powerfully dwell inside me today.*
  *I place my dear coach Kimmer in your hands. I
desire to see you work mightily in his life, for your
name's sake. Let him be open to my letter & open
with me. Bring walking Christians in his life to
nudge him along. I pray for his mom, for her
health & salvation. May you show Kimmer that
you are the most imp. thing. Help him with his
team. I pray that I can encourage them.*

I pray for *Lisa* & *Megan* today. May you be with them. Give them peace & comfort.

And of course, I am going to be persistent. *Please* be with my husband, make him the man you desire. *Break* him down. *Allow* him to see you today. *Prepare* us for one another. I pray for your perfect timing to meet & begin growing with you in the center. I need that and desire that, but I know I can be content with you. *Help* me to be patient, my *Lord*.

—KP

3/4/93

Lord,

Thank you for this awesome day. I thank you for all of the beauty surrounding it. It is so lovely, my *Lord*. *Be* with Coach Carp today. I don't know why I feel so strongly to pray for him. May *Kimmer* find you in the way you desire. I put our friendship in your hands, I trust you with my heart & motives. *May* he see me for who I am and vice versa. *He* has quality written all over him. May I see his spiritual side, and may you build that up for your sake & your glory.

3/6/93

Lord Jesus,

Be with Kimmer today. I often ask why he is on my mind and pressed on my heart. Help me to be a witness with him, let me see what you mean to him. I do enjoy getting to know him. He's a quality feller, but if he doesn't know you & <u>desire</u> to grow with you, his life is meaningless. May he receive my letter & your words very openly. May you continue to help him coach above reproach. Keep my thoughts pure always & keep temptation distant.

How I long to love my husband someday & have his children. How I desire to be a supportive wife and a witness to those around us. How I desire to share God's love, your love, with other couples. I want to be used by you. Please show me what you desire.

I pray for Kimmer's mom—may she really know you & may she continue to be restored in health. Be with NMHU's team. Help them to play well. Bring Christians to Kimmer—may he be grounded in you for your glory. Thank you for our friendship. We have so many things in common, but I need to know if we have the most imp. one. In some ways I

feel he does because he believes. I can relate, but
there is so much more. Please use me as a tool—
Holy Spirit, please guide & direct me.
　　—KP

3/12/93
Dear Lord Jesus,
　　Thank you for everything you have given me. I
pray that I could be a good witness to those around
me who don't know you. I pray for your Holy
Spirit to fill me up and guide me.
　　Lord, I really need your wisdom & Spirit to guide
me with Kimmer. I am going to be honest with
you. Part of me really likes the person that he is. It's
fun to see that you are so special to him. I want to
know how personal you are to him. For some reason I just see a heart for you there—a quality man, a
deep heart and a heart of gold. I pray you would
show me which direction to go. I would love to see
you work and make this humble heart dependent
on you & give his life over to you if he has not. Part
of me wants to meet him—I think it would be fun.
Part of me doesn't because I don't want to begin to
have feelings for him if this is not of you. If it is, I

pray you would show me that. I want to be led by you. I see so many ways in which we relate, but you must be the center.

I would love to talk about these things with him, but I pray he brings them up in your timing. I pray for our friendship if you want it to continue. I pray that you would lead me if it is OK if I go see him—I want to take one day at a time. Please Lord, I pray for Kimmer, if his team plays this weekend, I pray for a win. Lord, show Kimmer he needs you. Put a desire in his heart to seek you. Lord, I lay this down at your feet. Please guide me, Father.

—KP

3/15/93

Lord,

Today I need you more than ever. How thankful I am for you. How I long to be guided by you and know that your Holy Spirit is in control of my life. Please Father, guide me into all truth. I feel so consumed with many different things it's almost overwhelming at times. I do think of Kimmer. I don't know why, but I will pray for him steadfastly. I do pray that I will know if he has a personal relationship with the Lord. With you, God. I pray you are working in his life. I pray that you will be working in my life as well. Please show me what your will is and what you desire of me. I don't see anything wrong with writing letters & talking as long as he knows where I am coming from.

—KP

3/17/93

I don't know why I have this sense to keep Kimmer in prayer, but if this is your will, may you continue to burden my heart. Lord, guide our friendship. May it continue to be open and growing if this is your will. Sometimes I would love to see you do something dramatic & awesome with our friendship. Of course it is highly unlikely, but you can do anything, more than what we can think of or imagine. I'm just asking you to guide our friend-ship, let me be a witness & example. Show me if I am not being the woman you desire. Show me clearly if I should meet him in N.M.

—KP

3/18/93

Eph. 3:20–21 "Now to Him who is able to do exceeding abundantly beyond all that we ask or think, according to the power that works within us, to Him be the glory in the church and in Christ Jesus to all generations forever and ever. Amen."

Thank you, Lord Jesus, for who you are—thanks for giving me hope, peace, and comfort. I pray that you would guide me according to your ways. To you Lord I lift up my voice, knowing that you do understand me better than anyone. I do pray that I can be an example to Kimmer, Lord. I pray for Coach Carp Lord. You are obviously breaking him down. I ask that you put some godly people to surround him. Let him ask me questions & others too. Let him see his purpose for his existence. I thank you for our friendship. He is very fun to talk to and I do enjoy getting to know him. I pray, Lord, for his personal growth. I pray, Lord, that you would convict his heart. May he be open to me please & most of all you—accepting you, Lord. I think it's funny to think that if you wanted, you could have something happen with our friendship—I love to see you work, and it's my desire to see you work in his life in a mighty way, knowing that you burdened me for him.

I know you know where my husband is. Please be with him now—comforting him. Help me, Lord, to draw near to you. Please, Holy Spirit, guide me according to you always. I love you.

—Krisxan

3/26/93

Dear Lord,

It's 2:00 A.M. and I just talked to Kimmer for about one hour on the phone. It was good to talk to him, and I am so frustrated for him too. I pray, Lord, that you would really come alongside of him & encourage him. I pray, Lord, that you would give him the patience that he needs. Help him to encourage his team, Lord, the way that they need to be encouraged. I thank you for watching over them on their bus ride. Please protect them. I pray for their games tomorrow that they would go well. They need you, Lord Jesus. May your Spirit continue to be working in his life.

We have such a funny friendship. I really enjoy it and he is so fun to talk to. I'm glad that he knows he can talk to me & I will listen. I pray that you would continue to show me if it's OK to go visit him. May I continue to know & see more about him. Some of the qualities I see in him I do like. It's nice to talk about you. I pray that you would help show him what your priorities for him are, Lord. I trust you with our friendship, Lord. I do trust that you are working, Father. Please, Lord, be in control of my heart & my thoughts. May you lead me & show me what is right. May Kimmer & I continue to have good conversations.

Please guide our friendship & our hearts—I am trusting you big time.

[no date]

Isaiah 26:4 "Trust in the LORD forever, for in God the LORD, we have an everlasting Rock."

Lord,

I thank you and praise you for Kim. I thank you for the way our relationship has developed. It's pretty incredible the way you have made the doors open up and for us to develop an intimate relationship with each other. There is no one else like him. I know that. He seems like the perfect one for me.

Help me, Lord, to lay this down at your feet. Help me to look to his heart & what <u>you</u> say, not the approval of man. Show me, Lord; continue to make my heart's desire your desire. Give me the peace that is everlasting, the contentment that remains. Show me if Kim is the one for me. <u>In my heart I feel, Yes.</u>

You know us spiritually. Blend our hearts together, help us individually to seek after you. Help me to know when to tell him that I <u>love</u> him. Show me; work with my heart & mind. I pray for Kimmer—give him strength, make him desire fellowship, growth, disciples—I know you're faithful, Lord. Help me to grow closer each & every day to you & then to him. I love you.

—Krickitt

5/27/93

Show Kimmer & me your perfect timing. Continue to draw me near to you & fall in love with him more & more. Please protect him & keep him strong & safe. Fill his heart if it feels empty or lonely. Help him play great in his golf tourney. I pray that we would be a great witness for you—

please protect us and keep us safe. I love you—Let Kimmer know how much I adore him. Thank you, Lord Jesus.
—Krickitt

July 22, 1993
Lord Jesus—
Wow! How my life has been blessed. I am so excited about Kimmer's & my wedding plans. I thank you & praise you for how you have truly opened the doors wide open for us. Thank you for allowing everything to fall right into place. Thanks for Mom & Dad and everyone that is helping out. I am so blessed. Be with me today—fill me with your Holy Spirit. Keep my mind free, clean & pure—it's a total battle right now. I need your help.

Today may I put on your full armor and walk in the power of your Holy Spirit. Forgive me of my ways, help me to have pure thoughts, resist temptation, and purify my heart through & through. May the time between now and our wedding go by fast and not drag. Help me to get all the things accomplished that I need to. Remind me of the little things that must be completed. May you help me today to be a witness and example for you. I love you very much.

   —Krisxan

   August 22, 1993

   Dear Lord—

   One month from today I will be Mrs. Kim J. Carpenter. I can hardly believe it! Wow. I wanted to thank you, Lord, for all of my many blessings. You <u>have</u> done far more than I could have ever dreamed, and thank you. Please prepare me to be the woman of God—that godly wife that you deserve for me to be. Let me have confidence because of you. Prepare both of us for our new life that is to come. Many changes coming up I'm sure. Be with Kimmer. Please provide the players he needs for this year. I pray, Lord, that you would have mercy on his team and help them to have a great season. They need you very much. I pray that this time will go quickly. Help us to get all the things done that we need to. Without you, we can't do it. Be with everyone in the wedding party. Keep them safe & allow them to get all their stuff done. We need your help. I love you, Lord. May I make you proud today. —Krisxan

August 29, '93, <u>20 days!!</u>

Dear Lord,

I thank you so much for blessing me with a beautiful bridal shower yesterday. It was so nice to see old friends who are dear to me. I pray, Lord, that you will begin preparing their hearts to hear your gospel on the day of our wedding. It is my prayer that our day is glorifying to you and people may see our love for you through our wedding. Please be with Kimmer today. Help him to find rest today. I pray that you will help him with all of his stress & he will be able to give <u>you</u>, Lord, his burdens. May he grow closer to you & spend quality time with you—growing in his relationship with you. May we both grow closer to you and may you take the little details of my day & help me to get them accomplished. Thank you for all you have given me. I need you each and every day. I love you —Krisxan

Sept 9, 1993

Dear Lord,

I want to thank you for only nine more days until our wedding. It seems like it has been a long haul—even though we have thankfully only had a three-month engagement. Thank you for Kimmer and his wonderful heart. I thank you for his patience with me and his willingness to be a great husband.

I thank you for my man. I pray for our marriage. I thank you for our church and the opportunities for ministry there. I am really excited for what you are going to do. Please burden my heart and give me a <u>desire</u> for what you desire me to do. Help me to remain dependent on your Spirit. I pray for the rehearsal & the wedding day, that everything may go smooth. Please continue to encourage me and work in us as your children. Help us to be an example & witness of your love and a God-centered marriage. We need you. I love you & need you. Please walk with me, Lord.

—Krisxan Carpenter (to be!)

[no entries between 9/9 and 11/24]

11/24/93

Lord—

Thank you for all you do for me. Thank you for the opportunity we get to go home for

Thanksgiving today. Help us to have endurance to work hard for your values. I pray for opportunities to serve you, be a witness for you, be a leader for you. I do want to be open for your work. Please open my heart and Kimmer's to do the things that will be pleasing to you. Thank you that I am your temple, and that I have so much because of you. Thank you for my wonderful husband. I need him & love him. Love forever.

—Krisxan Carpenter

My official photo as Coach Kim Carpenter of the Highlands Cowboys. Krickitt said the uniform made me look like a little boy.

Krickitt and Kristi Pinnick were gymnasts together at Desert Devils Gymnastics Club. Krickitt then went on and received a full gymnastics scholarship at Cal State Fullerton.

With help from her roommates, I sneaked up and surprised Krickitt under this balcony to propose.

Our engagement photo. The matching outfits recall our first meeting—on the phone discussing an order for athletic jackets.

Mr. and Mrs.
Kim J. Carpenter,
September 18, 1993.

The wedding party. Some of these friends and family would soon play a part in our lives we couldn't possibly have imagined.

Honeymooning on Maui the first time. Krickitt will never remember it; I will never forget it.

What was left of our car after a collision the night before Thanksgiving 1993. This angle shows the crushed driver compartment and the sunroof that sliced up my back.

This angle shows where rescue workers cut the roof and door apart to get Krickitt out. The car landed upside down, and she hung suspended by her seat belt for more than half an hour.

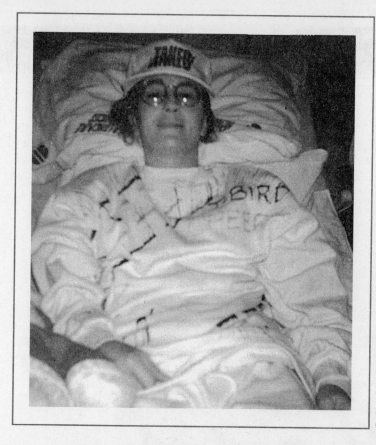

Krickitt at Barrow Neurological Center in Phoenix, Christmas 1993. The fact she was alive was a miracle; at this point we didn't know what level of recovery to expect.

Krickitt, her sister-in-law Gretchen, and brother Jamey at Barrow, January 1994. Jamey and Gretchen were strong spiritual supporters during Krickitt's rehab.

Krickitt with her mom, Mary Pappas, about two months after the accident. Krickitt had graduated to outpatient status.

Krickitt and me in the courtyard at Barrow with my parents, Danny and Mo Carpenter.

Scott Madsen, Krickitt's "physical terrorist," became a real friend who helped me keep my perspective during the inevitable setbacks in her therapy.

Clowning around trying to get reacquainted, February 1994.

Hiking the summer after the accident. Behind the smiles, our relationship was coming apart. Divorce was never an option, but there were times we thought we could never live together again under the same roof.

Krickitt and her family at the North Eastern Regional Hospital rehab center where she worked before the accident, back on the job in the summer of '94. That's Gretchen, Grace, and Jamey up front, with her parents and me in back.

Building new memories.

Getting to know each other again while visiting Krickitt's parents in Phoenix.

Our second wedding ceremony, May 25, 1996, at a remote mountain chapel in New Mexico. It didn't even have electricity, but the view was awesome.

We had agreed to use our original wedding rings in the second ceremony. But each of us secretly bought a second ring for the other, so we had four rings to juggle.

The second wedding party, facing a throng of reporters and photographers from the London *Times, Inside Edition, People* magazine, *Day and Date,* and other media. For keeping our original wedding vows, we'd become celebrities.

At the reception after the second ceremony, three key players in our story: Scott Madsen, Krickitt's physical therapist; Marcy Madsen, recreational therapist; and Bob Grothe, flight nurse.

Krickitt's dad, Gus Pappas, with DJ Coombs, the EMT who overcame her own claustrophobia to climb into our wrecked car and treat Krickitt while she was still trapped inside.

Our second honeymoon in Maui.

In Maui our second time around, strangers recognized us on the street, and a California radio station woke us up at 4:00 A.M. for a live interview.

Backstage in New York with Krickitt's parents and Maury Povich.

Relaxing in Arizona at the Miraval Resort, compliments of *The Leeza Show.*

Enjoying God's great miracle—a new life together.

Chapter 8
AT THE FOOT OF
THE CROSS

ay after day Krickitt kept up her outpatient treatment program at Barrow, and week after week I made the trip from Las Vegas to Phoenix to be with her and encourage her during therapy. I still pushed her harder than her physical therapist—her "physical terrorist"—did. The husband in me had grown dormant and the coach had taken over. We were no longer husband and wife but student and coach.

Far from appreciating my cheering her on, she hated it more than ever. There were times when she was quiet and agreeable, but my prodding her to do more and do it better provoked screams and swearing. She was completely unguarded with her speech and her opinions about things, acting and reacting like a child.

The doctors had warned me that she could be very uninhibited, and there were times when uninhibited only began to describe her. Even when there were people in the room, she'd grab me without any warning and say in a stage whisper, "Hey, let's be naughty." Then when I resisted she said, "You don't love me any more. You don't love me because I'm crippled!" I wanted to love her, but it was too strange emotionally—more like making love to my daughter than to my wife.

At this point her doctors thought a visit to our apartment in Las Vegas might jog Krickitt's memory of me and our relationship. Her mom flew with her from Phoenix to Albuquerque, and my parents picked them up at the airport there. Then, full of hope and high spirits, they drove them to the apartment. Would the light finally click on? Would she suddenly be the woman I married again?

When I got home at the end of the day, Krickitt was friendly but really didn't seem to have any idea who I was. Her mom said that when they arrived the two of them walked around the living room, looking at the furniture, the pictures on the walls, the books in the bookshelf. There had been no emotion whatever in her face. She stood in the middle of the room and looked around. Nothing. A blank slate.

She asked what her china pattern looked like. She had chosen the pattern after a lot of shopping around and getting advice from her mother and friends. Her mom handed her a plate. She lifted it close to her face, then set it down again.

"That's nice," she said simply. As the tour continued, I quizzed her gently about different things around the apartment I thought might ring a bell: pictures of the two of us, furniture we'd picked out together. None of it registered. She was a stranger here.

Her doctors had asked me if we had a video of our wedding. I said we did, and they suggested that watching it might trigger something in Krickitt's memory about her married life. I asked her if she wanted to see the tape of our wedding, and she said yes.

The whole ceremony had been recorded. We sat on the couch together and watched it from beginning to end: the crowds of friends, the elegant clothes, the candlelit church, the hilarious reaction when her dad tossed me the baseball, and the high-spirited recessional.

Somehow I sensed that she knew how important her remembering was to me, and she tried to be encouraging.

"I recognize that girl—that bride—in the video as me," she said thoughtfully, "but I don't have any connection with her. I don't know what she's thinking and feeling. I see she's a bride, and I see you standing there with her, and the two of you exchanging vows. It's like watching a friend on video. I don't know what the girl on the screen is thinking." There was no emotion in her voice. No feeling in her heart.

After a few days she went back to the outpatient program in Phoenix, and I went back to my grueling routine, spending Monday through Thursday with Krickitt and the rest of the week with the team at Highlands or on the road.

Alone back in Las Vegas, I called Krickitt every day we were apart. One afternoon her mom mentioned that Krickitt had told the therapist she "missed that guy who calls and hangs around." She remembered my visits and was starting to refer to me as "that guy" all the time. One night I didn't call, and the next day Krickitt asked her mom if she could call me.

When Mary Pappas called, I was ecstatic. She put Krickitt on the line.

"Hi, this is Krickitt." Pause.

"Krick, this is Kimmer. I'm really glad you called."

More silence. Then, "Hi, this is Krickitt. Well, I gotta go now. Good-bye."

She felt something for me down deep, but she just couldn't put the pieces together when we got on the phone. This was the first of many times she'd call, say a sentence or two, and hang up.

A couple of weeks later I was in Phoenix working away at therapy with Krickitt. After we were finished, Scott Madsen, the "physical terrorist" who had become such an important part of Krickitt's recovery, asked me if I'd like to help him coach a boy's basketball team that afternoon. Grateful for a break in the routine, I said I'd like to.

Our time together was a godsend. For two hours I completely forgot about having a wife who didn't know who I was, having medical bills stacked to the ceiling, and being completely exhausted every day and every night of my life. I got caught up completely in the strategy of the game and helping Scott's team come out on top.

The funny thing is that looking back, I can't remember whether we won or lost. That's because of what happened later in the day that was an even greater gift from God.

Scott suggested we have a soft drink after the game, and so the two of us sat down at the snack bar. After a little coaches' debriefing about the game, he paused briefly, looked at the table for a moment, then up at me.

"I know you're getting discouraged about Krickitt," he said. "I honestly don't know how you keep going."

He knew the truth, so there was no point in hiding it. "It's tough. Really tough," I admitted. "Sometimes I get so jazzed when I think we're about to have some kind of breakthrough, when I think she remembers something that would link us together. Then she cusses me out for pushing her too hard in therapy—or for no reason at all—and it tears my heart out. It's the toughest coaching job I've ever had."

"We can keep on helping Krickitt," Scott continued. "Physically she's making incredible progress. If she hadn't been in such good condition because of her gymnastics, she'd never have made it this far. But you're important too. Krickitt needs somebody strong, confident, and forgiving; you've got to be that to her, but you can't do it by yourself. You've got to have God."

"You're right," I said. "But it's tough to think that way when just getting through the day seems impossible."

"God hasn't forgotten you," he said with quiet confidence. "God will never forget you. He says he will never leave you comfortless, and he won't. You can't use him up or wear him out. Hang on to him, Kim. He's the most powerful force for good you've got. He won't forget you. Don't you forget him."

Lying awake at the Pappas house late that night, I thought over and over about Scott's advice. Maybe I'd forgotten to put my troubles at the foot of the cross. Maybe in all the exhaustion and desperation I had overlooked the most powerful tool of all for Krickitt's recovery. However often or sincerely I prayed, I knew I could do better. However much I trusted in God, my trust could be deeper. I promised God then and there I would always remember him and never shy away from praying to receive the awesome power he commands.

That night reminded me of the way I'd felt at the hospital in Albuquerque when Krickitt's cranial pressure was going through the ceiling and we didn't know whether she would live or die. During the course of those first uncertain hours, I had felt myself gradually but steadily giving Krickitt's life over to Christ. The more I trusted in him, the more at peace I felt, even though I knew he might take her any moment. Scott's wise words were like a refresher course in putting my faith in God's ability instead of in my own.

From time to time there were tantalizing signs that Krickitt was continuing to improve. One day in March, her mom called with the news that she had been in her old bathroom in Phoenix, looking in the mirror at the place where her skull had been dented in the wreck. She touched it as she looked, feeling around it with the tips of her fingers.

"Hmmmmm," she said. She seemed mildly curious about the injury. "Maybe I really did have this accident."

Ever since she came out of her coma, she'd kept telling us she felt like she was in a dream that we were all part of. She insisted she never had a wreck, never had been married, was trapped in a nightmare, and knew she would eventually wake up. Her reaction in front of the mirror was the first solid indication that she had some idea her dream world might be real after all.

It was a promising sign and an answer to prayer, but her next trip to Las Vegas later that month was anticlimactic. She came back to our apartment and looked around like before. She wasn't as lost or disoriented, but that was because she remembered it from her last trip, not because she ever remembered living there with me. We went through the same motions: looking at the china she'd picked out, looking at wedding pictures and the wedding video. She seemed to like it all right, but nothing helped her really connect with her past.

I think this was the first time there was ever any news coverage about us. The Friday Krickitt came to Las Vegas, the local *Daily Optic* ran a story in the sports section about the Cowboys game that weekend and how Krickitt would be the most important fan in the crowd as far as the team's coach was concerned.

"Before the accident we were caught up in the will to win," they quoted me as saying. "It took something devastating like this to make me realize that winning is not everything. Until you go through something like this, you don't understand. My outlook on life in general has changed. You tend to respect life a lot more. My priorities are a little different." And how.

Krickitt's mom had traveled with her once again, and at the airport on their way back to Phoenix she stopped a few steps away from us at the gate so Krick and I could have a private moment to say good-bye.

I held her face in my hands. She was so beautiful.

"I love you, Krickitt," I said.

"I love you too." Her mouth spoke, but her eyes said nothing. She gave me a quick noncommittal hug like I was her third cousin. As we embraced, I glanced at my mother-in-law across the waiting area. I could see the same aching, overwhelming disappointment in her expression that I felt inside.

Dr. Singh and the rest of the Barrow team set a tentative date of April 14 for Krickitt's release from the outpatient program. In spite of her memory loss, Krickitt was excited about getting back to Vegas. Though she still lashed out at me without any warning, we were building—or rebuilding, I couldn't tell yet—a relationship together. She didn't accept me as her husband, but she missed me now on days I didn't call or visit. There were times when she enjoyed being with me and we really seemed to be getting somewhere. I held tight to those moments and frantically tried to figure out what made them work.

As April 14 approached, Krickitt and I both felt the strain of not knowing for sure whether they would allow her to come back to Las Vegas. They took note of her astonishing progress, and reported that "she is very eager to return to her husband in New Mexico." She still had some physical limitations and still couldn't qualify to get her driver's license back yet —there were more hurdles there, including intermittent vision problems. But in the end everybody signed off, and on April 14, 1994, Krickitt came home.

Four days later we celebrated our seven-month anniversary. Krickitt had spent two-thirds of our married life as a hospital patient.

As much as I had tried to prepare myself for Krick's reentry into life at home, it didn't take long to realize our life together was a disaster in the making. We couldn't relax around each other. Even though she had missed me at Barrow, she still didn't accept me as her husband and didn't remember how we lived before the accident.

Shortly after she got home, I found her standing in the middle of the kitchen with a confused look on her face.

"Hey Krick, what's the matter?" I asked.

After taking a minute to formulate the words, she said, "How did I do the wife thing?"

I asked her what she meant.

"You know, the wife thing. Did I cook for you? Did I make you lunch? Did I wave to you when you left in the morning? I don't know what I'm supposed to do. I'm so confused."

I held her close. Her hair smelled like flowers. She looked up at me.

"I know I'm supposed to be married to you. I know I like you and miss you when you're gone." A pause, and then, "I know you've been so faithful. You're always there when I need you. I know these things. I know them. But I don't know I'm married to you. I wish I did, but I don't."

"I love you, Krickitt."

"I love you too."

I had to leave her in the apartment when I went to school. She'd been able to fool the hospital security system, and I worried that if she went out for a walk she could get lost.

"Promise me you won't run off and get lost," I said.

"I promise," she answered softly, the picture of contrition.

But only a day or two later, we got into an argument and she was gone. I found her down the street on the pay phone with her mom.

"You promised me you wouldn't run away," I said firmly.

"I can't promise you anything!" she shouted, then ran into the bedroom and slammed the door.

"Krickitt!" I shouted.

"GET AWAY! I HATE YOU!" She screamed like an animal, then I heard her dissolve into heaving sobs of frustration and rage. I walked away and waited for her to calm down.

And so it went: times of companionship and rebuilding, interrupted by the temper outbursts of an unruly teenager; times when she completely lost control, separated by times when she was as frightened and confused about her behavior as I was.

At least I had stopped my weekly commute to Phoenix. That gave me the chance to settle back into my coaching duties and concentrate on building a winning team. I needed something winning in my life like I'd never needed it before.

But by now there was nowhere I could go to get away from the pressure. I was too tired and stressed to be the coach my team needed and deserved. My home life was in ruins: Krickitt was continuing to improve mentally, but our relationship was going nowhere. Our sex life varied between hopeless and impossible. We were living together but not living as husband and wife. It was still more like father and daughter.

Krickitt lost her temper over everything. She couldn't remember where she put things around the house. She couldn't seem to go a whole day without breaking something. She got tired easily and got bored with staying at home all the time because she couldn't drive. In conversations with me or other people, she would laugh when she meant to cry, and interrupt me or one of our friends in mid-sentence to blurt out a long story on a completely different subject.

I was living with two women inside one body. One was kind and gentle and doing all she could to rebuild our married life. The other was a sullen teenager with a flash temper who knew her words could cut me and loved watching me bleed.

I knew she was still in pain because I was, and she had been injured a lot worse than I'd been. My back was still giving me trouble, but my worst problems at this point weren't physical. I'd been diagnosed with post-traumatic stress disorder. That, the doctors said, was one of the main reasons I couldn't sleep at night and why I was so tense and stressed all the time. So I could make it from one day to the next, they gave me antidepressants, prescription painkillers, and heavy-duty sleeping pills.

Then there were the bills. And the collection agencies. And the lawyers. From the time they'd started calling when Krickitt was still in a coma, various health-care providers and their collection agencies had kept up a steady stream of phone calls and letters. Our total liability for Krickitt's care was just under $170,000. With my bills and a car to replace the Escort, the total was a little over $200,000. The other driver had no insurance, so everything depended on our own auto insurance company. And they were still playing hardball.

I felt the walls closing in and like I was powerless to do anything to regain control of my life. The whole thing was more than I could handle. But it wasn't too much for God. As he had so many times over the past few months, he came to my rescue.

I shouldn't be surprised that God showed me what to do. What was surprising to me, though, was the messenger he picked for the job.

Rob Evers was not only my boss as athletic director at New Mexico Highlands University; he was also a good friend. He had encouraged me to spend time with Krickitt in Phoenix and had kept my job open for me even when I had no idea when or whether I'd be back. He'd watched me struggle during the weeks of commuting between Las Vegas and Phoenix, and he watched now as I battled on against increasing odds while still trying to coach his baseball team.

One afternoon early in the fall of 1994, Rob asked me to come into his office and told me privately he thought I needed counseling.

"Krickitt's the patient, not me," I insisted.

"I'm not worried about Krickitt. She's got plenty of doctors and therapists watching her progress. She's had the best therapy available. Most of all, Kim, she's got you to love her and look after her. Who's looking after you?"

"I'm going to be all right," I said. "Things are getting better. Krick's coming along, and I'm fine. Really."

He was unconvinced. "Kim, I've watched you with the team. Nobody questions your commitment to the team and your heart for baseball. But you need help. You need counseling, and you need it now. If you say no, I'm putting you on administrative leave."

I was getting my own dose of tough love.

He agreed to give me a few days to think it over. Of course he was right—I knew that on some level the minute he said it—only I didn't want to believe it. I wanted to be strong, to reclaim my place as a husband and head of the household; I didn't want to face the fact that I was losing ground with every passing minute. Besides, the last thing I needed was more medical bills. But a social worker assured me that the school's health insurance would cover it.

So I resigned as baseball coach. And right away I knew it had been the right thing to do. My job now was to take care of Krickitt. Still, with our lives so unsettled, even that decision had its downside. Krick and I were sitting together in the bleachers at the first game after I resigned, when a fight broke out on the field. Both benches cleared in a heartbeat, and the two teams formed themselves into a matted scrum of cleats and fists. The sight of it confused Krickitt and upset her. The coach of the opposing team told me in no uncertain terms that if I had been doing my job like I should have been, this never would have happened.

The summer after the accident, Krickitt had recovered enough to take a job fifteen hours a week as an exercise technician at the same hospital fitness center where she'd worked before the accident. The routine of going back to work three mornings a week and the chance for her to be in charge of something again were both good for her. She was on time for work and well prepared—there was a shadow of the old Krickitt in the slim young woman who helped people in the hospital's wellness center, surrounded by fitness equipment, weight machines, and free weights that had once been such a part of her life.

Yet for all the progress she made toward being self-sufficient, our relationship went from a rough ride into a death spiral. Just when I thought our home life couldn't be more erratic and stressful, Krickitt's flashes of hatred toward me got more brutal than ever.

I took Rob's advice and started seeing a therapist. At this point I had nothing to lose. By the end of 1994, Krickitt and I could hardly stay in the same room together without having a fight. We'd be having a normal conversation about some innocent topic or another, when something I would say set her off.

One day when we were visiting my parents, we went to get a car wash. Standing at the exit waiting for the car to come out and be dried off, we got into an argument. In only a few seconds we were screaming at each other. She took her water bottle and threw it at me, then took off down the sidewalk. I still couldn't move very fast, but I caught up with her in a minute or two in a fast-food restaurant, crying on the phone to her mom.

One particularly bad day in the middle of a rather animated disagreement, she picked a fork up off the table behind her, whirled around, and threw it. It stuck in the wall beside me.

"LEAVE ME ALONE! I HATE YOU!"

"Krickitt, get a grip!" I was furious. An inch to the left and that fork would have been sticking out of my shoulder instead of out of the wall.

"STOP TREATING ME LIKE A CHILD!"

"STOP ACTING LIKE ONE!!"

Her eyes burned with hatred. She turned down the volume but turned up the intensity. Staring at me like a wild animal, she hissed, "Maybe I should just slit my wrist."

I'd had enough. "There's a knife in the kitchen," I said, pointing in that direction.

"You think I'm kidding, don't you? Maybe I'll hang myself."

"There's a rope in the truck."

She bolted outside and slammed the door shut behind her. In the second it took me to yank it back open she had disappeared. She was the one with the brain injury, but now she was making me crazy. I found her later, exhausted and crying, hiding behind a car in the apartment parking lot.

We got back inside and sat down in the living room. There was a long silence.

"I miss the old Krickitt," I said at last.

"I miss her too," she answered.

That night after Krickitt was asleep, I played my mental video of our fight over and over in my head. This was the bottom. My wife didn't know who I was; I didn't know who she was; we were in debt up to our eyeballs; collection agencies were wearing me out; I couldn't sleep; I was taking too many pills; and I wasn't doing the university any good.

On occasion, well-meaning people had been asking me—indirectly but unmistakably—if I thought I might eventually throw in the towel and get a divorce. "There might be a time when you just have to let this go," they said. A social worker told me that when a married person has a debilitating head injury, the odds of divorce are around 80-90 percent. Taking that route would release me from my responsibility for her medical bills. It was an easy way out.

But for me the D-word was never an option. My answer was simple: "Nope. It will never happen." It didn't matter whether she remembered me or not, whether it took every penny I had to take care of her, or even whether we ultimately lived together or apart. The simple truth was that I couldn't see myself going through life without Krickitt.

But at the same time, I knew I couldn't go on with her like we were. The more she recovered physically the worse I felt, because at the same time she was getting well, we were growing more distant emotionally.

It reaffirmed a feeling I'd first had when Krickitt was still at Barrow, one that had been weaving in and out of my thoughts for months, but something I'd hesitated to mention to anybody: the realization that my responsibility was not necessarily to reestablish our household as husband and wife the way it once was. It might never happen. Instead, my job as a husband who truly, selflessly loved his wife was to help restore her independence to the point where she could live the rest of her life on her own if that's what it took to bring her peace.

Chapter 9

KRICKITT'S DIARY 3—
"Help me not to lose it"

[Dictated three days after coming out of her coma to Julie Vander Dussen, a dear friend from her Bible study at Eve Free who said a prayer at our wedding in 1993]

12/18/93

Life is very good. Therapy is very confusing at times. I miss the way things used to be with steady Bible study and church meetings, but I know that's the way things are. The Lord is constantly teaching us. I know he has me in his right pocket and I'm very safe there. I love to see him really work in my life, and I know he'll use me in his due time. Life is very fun but confusing at times. It's very nice to relax and think about our Savior. Something significant happens every second, but life is so fast that it passes me by at times.

3/20/94

Dear Lord,

I want to thank you so much for saving my life and intervening into our situation. Help me to be a witness of your work and glory. Please, Lord, help me to get back to the old Krickitt. I feel like I am almost there, but nowadays it is so hard to tell because I am critiqued for everything. Continue to strengthen me and help build Kimmer's and my marriage. May you continue to be the center of us. Guide our paths and open the doors to use us the way you want to. Have mercy on us, O Lord. Protect us please. You are so great and awesome. Please keep the enemy away from both of us. I bind him in Jesus' name. Help us to endure through the next month. Please help my memory and short-term memory and my fear. You are the Great Physician and you are the one I love and trust and turn to. Thank you, Lord. I love you and need you.

—Love, Krisxan Carpenter

3/26/94

Dear Lord,

I am in New Mexico and it feels so good to be back here with Kimmer. Please give me the strength to continue my therapy, and I pray that I will be released the 14th of April. I really want to be back with Kimmer and get our new life going again. I am relying on you to restore all of my feelings for our relationship. I ask that you will guide Kimmer on what he should do about coaching next year. May your will be done for his direction and our future.

Please Lord, I ask that your Great Physician's hand intercedes and cures his back so that he won't have any complications and that his nose will be protected by you. We need your help and guidance, Lord. Thank you for sparing our lives in the accident, and I ask that you will use us for your glory. Please strengthen our marriage and make it even stronger than it was in the beginning. Help us to grow closer together and we give you our trust and thanks. I love you, Lord, and need your strength this weekend. Please strengthen me and know that you're guiding my steps. May I become the girl I

was and the one you want me to be. Help me to remain faithful, devoted, and ever so caring.

—KC

3/28/94

Mark 8:34–35 "If anyone wishes to come after
Me, let him deny himself, and take up his cross, and
follow Me. For whoever wishes to save his life shall
lose it; but whoever loses his life for My sake and
the gospel's shall save it."

Oh! This is true, Lord. Thank you so much for
this nice time together with Kimmer. I pray, Lord,
that you will be with Kim and truly show him
what you desire for him to do next year. Give him
an open heart, and a clear perspective. Help me to
be the supporting wife that you desire. I need you,
Lord, to make it day by day. Please continue to heal
my brain and make me the woman of God that
you desire. I love you, Lord.

—KC

3/30/94

Dear Lord,

As I am flying in an airplane, I am leaving behind my adorable husband once again. I thank you for him and how much fun we have together. I thank you for his continued faithfulness, and it is my prayer that you use this time to strengthen our marriage. It is my prayer, Lord, that I may, in fact, be released on the 14th of April. I can't wait to get settled in Vegas again, and please use us to make an impact for <u>you</u> in others' lives. It was interesting going to UNM hospital yesterday and meeting Dr. Adams & Sherry Kenna. May my recovery because of <u>you</u> make an impact on their spiritual lives. Sherry, the ICU nurse, said the reason they were letting so many people into my room is because I was scheduled to die. I was not supposed to live. Thank you, Great Physician, for saving my life. Help me to glorify you at therapy and help me return to the Krickitt that everyone knew & loved. Thank you for making me more compassionate and helping me to understand people who are going through storms. Please keep Kimmer & me through this one. We love you. I love you. —KC

5/9/94

Lord Jesus,

I thank you so much for being an awesome God who really does answer the prayers of his people. I thank you today for the warmth that I am feeling in my heart. I thank you for your Holy Spirit and the guidance he gives me. Please allow your Spirit to guide me. I thank you for comfort and peace during this stage of my life and this part of our marriage. You're the greatest. Please continue to guide and direct Kim and me. Show us what you would like us to get involved in, in the church. Also, I pray for a Bible study for us. Continue to help Kimmer to grow, seek you, and desire to spend more time with you. Help him to be the spiritual leader you want him to be. Thank you for his growth. I love you, need you, desire to know you.

Thank you for my life, and all of your many blessings. Please be with my family & friends and help them in these times of need. I love you.

—KC

6/2/94

Mark 9:23 "And Jesus said to him, 'If You can! All things are possible to him who believes.'"

Lord Jesus,

I thank you so much for really helping me, especially this last month that I have been home for good. I need you through each and every day, both Kimmer and I do. There are times that I am frustrated, depressed, and confused. Please help me during these low times. Even though they are low, I am still so thankful to be alive and I praise you for that. Help me to return to the Krickitt I was, in the ways you desire me to. I thank you for my health and recovery and pray that it will continue. Please be the center of Kim's & my marriage and help us to grow closer and closer each and every day. We need you and we love you. Thank you for loving us. Help us to have a great weekend together. Help strengthen me and bring back the verses and knowledge of you that I once had. Help me as I fear because of my lack of knowledge. I love you.

–KC

6/7/94

Ephesians 2:8–9 "For by grace you have been saved through faith; and that not of yourselves, it is the gift of God; not as a result of works, that no one should boast."

Dear Lord,

I thank you that I am saved, and that I have eternal life with you someday. I pray that you will continue to help me through the day. I can't believe all of the blessings and miracles you have done concerning me. I thank you. Also, I thank you for the most wonderful husband. I pray you will take and heal some of the pain he has in his back so that he can have energy to work through the day and spend time with you. Draw him near to you to have quiet times. May I continue to be an example to him. I pray for energy and dedication for him. Help him out in his low times. I pray for his depression, that you would help heal him and give him the inner strength that he used to have. I love you and thank you for everything. Watch over Mom, Dad, Gretchen, Jamey, and little Grace Ann. I love you, Lord, and need you. I love you.

—KC

6/19/94

Lord Jesus,

I just thank you so much for giving Kimmer &
me life. Life here on earth and eternal life with you. I
thank you that things are starting to come to a close
in this accident. Although it still is a long road, we
know that in time it will be over. I pray for our settlement that we would get a nice settlement so we
would be able to give to <u>you</u>. Also, please I ask for
your mercy on us that our insurance will accept the
amount and we will not have to go into arbitration.
May your will be done. Please help us, Lord. Help
Kimmer to be at peace with everything and may
you keep Mom and Dad safe. Help Kimmer and
me to be a witness to you. I ask for continued healing in my brain, my memory, and my personality.
Help me to return to me and act my age. Help us all
to have greater love in our hearts for each other and
you.

I pray for Kimmer. Help him to be a witness for
you. I pray, Lord, that you would help him so he
would be able to sleep again. Please. He is so exhausted. He needs rest from you. I pray that you
would help continue to heal his back, that it would

start to feel better. Thank you for the settlement amount. I pray that it will not be a long, long process.

Help me in my job to be a good witness for you and help my knowledge to return. I pray that my eyes are getting better and that they will continue to heal. Also Lord, I pray that you would be able to provide us with a neuro psych. I love you, Lord, and thank you. Help us to be *your* witness.

—KC

July 20, 1994, My 25th Birthday
Lord Jesus,

I just thank you so much for who you are and all that you do. It is my prayer that you will continue to help Kimmer and me and strengthen us according to your glorious might. Thank you for my life, and I give you glory for all that you do. I love you. Please help guide Kimmer with his job and show us your will where you want us. I pray that you could help us with finances and Kim's job. Also, I give our settlement to you. May you *please* shorten the process if it be thy will. I pray we get a good amount, so we can give to your kingdom. I

pray that they will accept my plea to get my driver's
license back. May you speed up the process if it be
thy will. May Kimmer and I have a special day together and may my physical desire return to normal please so I don't have to get counseling. I ask
that you really help me to give glory to you and
share you. Open hearts. Fill me with the words you
desire me to say.

  —KC

8/22/94

Isaiah 40:31 "Yet those who wait for the LORD
will gain new strength; they will mount up with
wings like eagles, they will run and not get tired,
they will walk and not become weary."

Lord,

I thank you so much for my life and all you do. I
pray that you help Kim & me become a godly couple. Help us both to have the _energy_ and grow spiritually toward you. Please Lord. I am so weary. I
ask that you pick me up and help me grow closer to
you. I pray that you will be with Kimmer. Give
him strength & energy today. Restore his health
back to what it used to be. If it be thy will, help him

to get his sleep & heal his back. I ask this in your name.

—Krick

10/18/94

Dear Lord,

I come before you today seeing my deep needs and insecurities due to our accident. I know in my heart you can help and provide help for me. I just pray and ask that you may guide me into the direction you desire not only for me but Kimmer too.

I love you Lord, need you, and thank you for all that you have done for me. You are the best. Please continue to help Kimmer and me in our marriage. Show us how to better meet the needs of each other. Help make Kimmer the spiritual leader that I need. Help him to have quiet times and have some sort of conviction when not spending time with you. And help me to stay faithful and get something out of my quiet times.

Please show us the path you desire us to go on and open and close doors. I pray for our settlement that you could work a true miracle amount-wise

and time-wise. I pray it may end <u>soon.</u> I have faith
& trust. It's in your hands; may your will be done.

I love & need you really bad myself right now.
Please continue to heal me and make me the Krick
I used to be in the way you desire. Help me to continue to try and stay positive and be a witness for
you. I pray I will regain the knowledge I once had
about you. Please protect Kim & me. I love you.
  —KC

10/25/94
Dear Lord,
I thank you so much for being by my side and
being so faithful to me. I need you now, and daily. I
can see that I <u>cannot</u> do this on my own strength,
but I need you to carry me and help me through
each and every day.

I pray for K & my marriage. Please be the center
of it and help us to treat one another with respect
and a lot of love. Help us to be good examples of a
godly marriage. I pray you help and strengthen
Kimmer to get through his hard & hectic schedule
with school and working. Give him rest, I ask.
Please help him to sleep better and find some rest.

I pray that if a counselor is to be found that you would lead us to him or her. Help me to return to the parts of Krickitt you liked. Please help me & forgive me with my frustrations. Love,
—KC

11/28/94
Dear Lord,
I thank you for being a God who understands and cares. I pray that you will continue to help me and heal me to be the Krickitt you desire. Be with Kimmer & I pray that you will really help him and answer his prayers. I pray for <u>hope</u> for him.

I love you, Lord. Continue to help heal me and restore my memory as clear as it used to be. I need you. Help me grow and fill my life. Help my fear level.
—Krisxan

12/14/94
Lord,
I come before you today, very thankful that you are one I can turn to who completely understands me. I pray that the desire to really grow with you

and spiritually with Kimmer will increase. I pray
that you put a desire in his heart to want to
earnestly seek you. I pray for someone to keep us
accountable and we keep them accountable.

Please, Lord, I beg of your mercy. Please continue to heal Kimmer and me and help us to return
to the people we were or that you desire us to be.
Guide us and show us <u>where</u> you want us next
year, and <u>what</u> road you desire us to travel down. I
pray that Kimmer will pursue his therapy. Show
me where to intervene and when not to. Convict him
when he doesn't follow through and isn't a man of
his word. I love you.

—Krick

2/12/95

Dear Lord,

Today I sit once again spending my Sunday
morning with you. I love you, and need you dearly.
I truly thank you that the mediation went good, even
though it is not over and it was quite hard on
Kimmer. I pray that you will miraculously speed up
the time of the date of the arbitration. I trust you with
that and ask that you truly will open Kim's heart

and show him how you desire all of this insurance stuff to be done. We truly put it all in your hands, knowing you will provide us with the best outcome.

Please help Kimmer & me to heal from this accident and recover to who <u>you</u> desire us to be. Help us to continue to grow in you and be godly people. Help us to get on with our quiet times.

We need you & love you deeply.

—K Carp

3/5/95

Dear Lord,

I thank you deeply for this time for me to relax and sit at your feet. I thank you that you have brought me as far as you have. Thank you for my dear husband and how much he means to me. I pray that you will continue to strengthen our marriage and draw us closer together & closer to you.

I pray that Kimmer will become the spiritual leader that <u>you</u> desire and I need. I pray I will fulfill my wife duties to the best of my ability. I pray that Kimmer will deeply desire to spend time with you. Burden our hearts to spend time with you & convict us if we don't spend the time we should.

I ask that you will forgive me of my sins and for-give me when I get real bitchy. Forgive me for the ways I behave and help me to control my anger. Help me, Lord. I pray you will lighten my heart and wash me clean with your blood. Help me as I am struggling through the loss of feelings from this accident. If there is any way and your will, I pray that I could remember them. I place all of these re-quests in your hands.

—KC

4/7/95

Well, Kimmer and I are in a fight. I feel like re-taliating right now. I know you are with me, Lord. Please show him how he can help me. Please con-vict him in the areas that I talked to him about, and show him if this is what you see as well. It may not be right because I am brain damaged, but I feel it is right. I put this all in your hands. I need your help.

—Krick

5/1/95

I really need you, Lord. I know that you are the one that lifts me up, picks me up, and understands me the very most. I pray that you help *Kimmer* and me in our marriage. Open his eyes to see that I need him and that our relationship needs some watering. I pray that you will help me to be secure in you. I know you are always here to lift me up and pull me out.

5/22/95

Dear Lord,

I thank you for who you are and how you are by me always. I need you and love you so much. Please take control of my life and guide *Kimmer* and me and show us which direction to go and what to do. I place our marriage in your hands and ask that you strengthen us together as a unit and bring back the feelings and love we had pre-accident—if that is your desire. I really ask that <u>you</u> would fill me with hope, joy, and love and help me to be the old me if that is what you desire. I need you. I pray Lord that you would lift my heart and warm it up. Please have mercy and gentleness on me. I love you.

—*Krickitt*

7/1/95

Lord, I need you so badly. I cannot go on in this life without you, I know that. Please draw near to me and strengthen & comfort me. I need help in my walk/journey with you, our marriage, our settlement, my hope & direction. I pray that you will be Lord with Kimmer & me. <u>We</u> cannot do it without you. Show us better how to serve you together and apart, and serve each other. Convict us in marital differences. Please let me be heard with him. Help him see his stubbornness. I am really discouraged right now. I haven't had this sadness in awhile, but I know that you can give me hope. Help us.

May your light shine & your grace cover us. I <u>love</u> & <u>need</u> you so <u>desperately</u>, Lord.

KC

8/31/95

Dear Lord,

Please forgive me for my sins. My life feels like it's in shambles right now. I give our marriage all to you. Please help us so that we can make amends. Please convict Kimmer in the way he needs to be for me & please help me to be the woman & wife he needs me to be. I feel that my wacko-ness is getting better but I have been in rage with my temper. I don't feel that he really cares all that much. Please forgive me and help me to be totally yours. I know I need to spend more time with you. Forgive me for my sins—help me to come clean. I feel so bad, sinful, & at a loss. I am turning to you to mend our marriage. I put our marriage in your hands. I need you. We need you. Help us, please.

9/3/95

Lord,

As I sit and think of all that my life has been involved in the last two years, it is utter amazement. I really have been carried a long way by you & I thank you for that. I continue to trust you and ask that you carry me on your shoulders as I walk this walk.

I need you. I feel really low right now. I ask that you would comfort my heart and continue to mend my spirit that has been crushed since Kimmer & I got in our fight. Please open his eyes to how my spirit is being crushed. I need your help.

I pray for Kimmer's walk & mine too. Help us to have the desire & conviction to spend time with you daily. We need you.

I pray for our marriage. Help strengthen us, deepen our love, and put the feelings back in both of us. Continue to guide us and show us what your perfect & pleasing will is. Comfort me as I trust you.

1/9/96

Lord,

I am so frustrated. I feel like Kimmer is trying to be my teacher. I don't need that. He just fully went off and was so disrespectful to me. I ask that you help show the two of us. I ask you for your forgiveness if I was impertinent. I pray you will forgive me & convict his heart if he acted inappropriately. I know that you are there for me. I need you. I feel under control right now for the most part. I ask that you help me and show us. I need a husband, not a teacher and not someone to disrespect me. Please help me to relax. I place this in your hands & this night in your hands.

Please help me not to lose it.

5/14/96

Lord,

I'm writing you this letter because I am frustrated and depressed and not happy with the way our marriage is. Yes, I know it is a life commitment, and I'm pleased with that. I just am not satisfied with our spiritual life as a couple. A prayer before dinner isn't cutting it. I am not fulfilled and I know that only you can truly meet my needs.

Please, I ask that your Spirit may truly touch me, and help me to be the spiritual wife & godly wife that you so desire. Our communication as a couple stinks. I pray that you will allow us to talk to each other. I think in Kimmer's heart he wants to be the husband I need and so desire & the one who made a vow to me 2-1/2 years ago, but I don't see it. I know in your perfect timing he is in there somewhere.

I'm frustrated, and at times I feel that Kimmer is too busy playing games with my feelings and emotions instead of just being there as a supportive husband. I think we both view the situation differently.

I want to be respected and treated as a wife of 26 years of age. I need that to feel complete and back *like an adult. I know it is hard for Kimmer, but I pray you will take him aside, open his eyes, and let him really see what it is that I need and deserve. Show me what I can do better for him.*

I desire the All-American husband he is in the media's eyes. I wish it could continue throughout the entire day when we fight all of the time, and I have never been in a relationship that has so much bickering. I know I have never been in a relationship with so many trials either.

Sometimes, actually a lot, I think that the next day I will mind my own business & do my own thing to avoid conflict with Kimmer, but I never do— thankfully. Becoming independent won't solve this problem. It will be ignoring the problem.

I wish I was really happy again. I'm asking you to restore that. I feel stripped and used, not fulfilled, Please meet me where I am at, but more so, meet Kimmer where he is at. Help him to be the husband that you so desire. I need You and am depending on You.

Help me Lord—Fill me.

—Krickitt

[second entry]

He told me tonight that he never looks at me in the eyes when we are talking. That hurt me so bad. I have a hard time believing that after I met him, Kim, in person, I would have fallen in love with him if he never looked at me during our conversations and gave me all of the attention.

See why the phone was great for Kim, he could do stuff & didn't have to look me in the eyes.

It is so painful to me to look at him while we are talking and he is always looking away. I can barely stand it. It is getting increasingly hard for me. I pray that you, Lord, will help in this area.

Also, I thought about it tonight. I don't know if I want my diamond earrings. They will mean not a lot to me. Just something Kimmer treated me with. Help me on this.

I have no peace right now. Kimmer probably has no clue how I am getting crushed. It is really hard times right now. Help us Lord. Restore us. Show me my old love.

Chapter 10

A SECOND CHANCE

I was living with a stranger. I had been so thankful to God for the miracle of Krickitt's recovery, and looked forward to her coming home with such joy and anticipation. To have my wife—my friend, my companion, my lover—with me again every day had been my constant prayer for months. I never dreamed the reality of her return could make me so frustrated and sad.

By the spring of 1995, I'd resigned myself to the fact that life would never be normal again and that the old Krickitt was not coming back. Continuing a now-familiar pattern, there were tantalizing glimpses of what I thought was the preaccident Krickitt—moments that pulled me in two directions at once. On one hand they returned me for a split second to the good old days; on the other they were heart-piercing reminders of the life I had lost.

The most encouraging part of Krickitt's recovery was that somehow her faith had remained intact. She had praised God and prayed to him shortly after being charted out of a coma. Later, when she was living with her parents during outpatient therapy at Barrow, she told her mother that she had a nagging feeling something was missing in her life. Her mom took her shopping for a prayer journal. That seemed to be the answer. As mixed up in the head as she was, she'd felt the absence of prayer in her life and wanted to make it a regular part of her routine again.

She never recovered her memory of our meeting, engagement, marriage, honeymoon, or anything of our life together. (Krickitt was not even fully aware of her unrecovered memory until a year and a half after the accident. She was extremely confused because she didn't know that she didn't know me.) But everybody kept telling her we were man and wife, and she'd watched the video of our wedding and looked at our honeymoon pictures a thousand times. That feeling she had as she looked in the mirror that time back in Phoenix stuck with her. Her life wasn't a bad dream she would eventually wake up from. It was the new reality. And as much as she rejected me sometimes, she had a sense that I was there as her protector and companion, and realized that I went out of my way to be with her and help her. "I figure if I fell in love with this guy before," she observed, "I guess I could do it again."

Her spiritual life seemed miraculously intact—as her brother, Jamey, had said early in her recovery, she had a rock solid "core of Christianity" that even this terrible experience couldn't damage. Could that faith be combined somehow with her faith in our marriage to close the gap between us or at least keep it from getting any wider?

One big mystery for me was still what Krickitt was thinking from one minute to the next. Her mood swings were so wide and unpredictable. *Unpredictable* described our whole relationship. What was her real personality now and how much of it was getting to the surface? How well was she communicating what she thought and felt inside? Were we seeing the new real Krickitt?

Maybe she knew how to behave, knew how to act with me, how to control her anger, how to be affectionate and forgiving, but couldn't put her knowledge into practice somehow because of her injury. Or maybe she had no idea about any of that. I didn't know what Krickitt was like spiritually and emotionally any more, and didn't know whether her true self—whatever that was—was represented in her actions, or whether there was a disconnect between what she thought and what she did.

Some reactions of hers surprised her as much as they did me. One day she asked me to rub her feet. I said I would, and she plopped them down in my lap—but accidentally so hard and in such a place that I experienced sudden and severe manly pain. It hurt so bad I threw up. At the sight of my distress, Krickitt started laughing and couldn't stop. Her reaction was tough for me, but it was frustrating for Krickitt too. I don't think she actually thought it was funny; she just couldn't control her emotional reaction. It was a typical response for head injury victims, and one more reminder of how far we still had to go.

Adding to the tension was the double-edged financial sword of relentless calls from collection agencies and the ongoing legal battle to settle with our auto insurance company, which was dragging its feet every inch of the way toward a payout. Up to the time of our accident, I'd never talked to a bill collector in my life. The only rubber check I ever wrote was because I once put a deposit into the wrong account by mistake. We had faithfully paid our premiums specifically to avoid a financial meltdown in the unlikely event of a serious accident. Now the meltdown had happened, and we were getting nowhere with our coverage.

Nowhere was another word that described my whole life with depressing accuracy at times. Some days the problems were overwhelming, sweeping over me like an ocean storm. I was drowning in stress and confusion and anger. I couldn't sleep, couldn't coach like I wanted to, didn't know how to be a husband to my wife any more.

Then other days life seemed less black and hopeless. The one rock for me then, the one lighthouse beam in the darkness, was faith. For all her gonzo behavior, I think Krickitt had faith, too, as much as I did. In the depths of our nastiest shouting matches, there was a tenuous thread that connected us somehow.

What could I do? One thing I had to do was get the counseling Rob Evers insisted on.

It felt weird to think of going to a counselor by myself after so many counseling sessions with Krickitt. At this point, though, I had nothing to lose. I had been sure I could hold myself together, nurture Krickitt along, and get us back on track. I'd worked at it for more than a year, and I had failed. We weren't getting anywhere. I had done all I could. I had to leave the rest up to God. I really think God needed to break me. I had to give everything to him. Lying in bed late one night with Krickitt asleep beside me, I came face-to-face once again with the fact that I was helpless without God and that only he could heal our marriage.

Staring at the ceiling, listening to the noises of the night, hearing and feeling Krickitt's relaxed, steady breathing beside me, I rolled these thoughts around in my head. *What was God doing with my life? What was he doing with my vow?*

I'd stood before God and a church full of people and promised to provide for and protect Krisxan "through times of challenge and need." To devote myself to her "every need and desire." To be faithful. I'd said those words with such joy and conviction. I had meant them then, and I would honor them now. I just didn't know how.

I called the state psychiatric hospital in town and made an appointment with a social worker. Rob hadn't given me anybody to ask for by name, so I took whoever was up next, I guess. Here again God stepped into my life in such an awesome way. A few days later I went for my first session and met Mike Hill, whose wisdom and insight would soon have an incredible impact on me. He was not your typical counselor. Nothing about him said "clinical" or "analysis" or anything stuffy or artificial. What you saw was what you got. He was friendly, open, and absolutely fearless.

I told him the whole story, ending with the realization that, while I would never divorce Krickitt, it would be difficult to live together happily, and that my best shot might be getting her to the point where she could be self-sufficient and live on her own.

He thought for a minute. "Why do you think Krickitt married you in the first place?" he asked.

"Because I'm funny, clever, and handsome," I quipped with a nervous laugh. Mike smiled and waited patiently. He was in no hurry, and he wasn't going to let me weasel out of an answer.

"Because of the way I treated her, I guess," I finally replied. "I was interested in her as a person first, not just as a girl to have a casual relationship with, and I think she liked that. We were soul mates before we fell in love. There's been a strong spiritual side to our relationship from the first. Krick has an awesome faith in Christ. The weekend we met we spent one whole evening reading Job together."

"How do you treat her now?"

"Like a father. Like a coach."

"So she feels like she's married to her father?"

It was my turn to smile. "You got me, Mike. I don't know how she feels. I know she's willing to accept that we're married because everybody keeps telling her we are. And I honestly think she wants to love me as her husband. But deep down, I don't think she knows who I am."

After taking some time to understand our situation, Mike suggested Krickitt come with me to one of our therapy sessions. She agreed, and her talk with Mike turned out to be an answer to prayer, the miraculous event Krick and I needed to start getting our lives back in sync.

We all understood Krickitt had lost her memory. What we didn't know was that, in spite of countless conversations throughout her rehab, Krickitt didn't understand what had happened to her. People kept telling her she was married to me, that she was in our wedding videos, that she had picked out the china in the cupboard of our apartment, and all the rest.

After she and Mike talked awhile, Mike said, "You know, Krickitt, I don't think you have any memory of meeting, dating, and marrying Kimmer." Incredible as it seems now, no one had ever said those simple words to her before.

Krickitt looked up with an excited start, her eyes shining like two blue diamonds. "That's it!" she said excitedly. "That's it! No wonder why this has been so weird."

We knew her memory had been erased. What clicked on now at last for her was the understanding that it was all right not to know me or recognize our china. She wasn't crazy or in a dream; she couldn't remember, because she had amnesia. It was nothing that was her fault.

She had kept thinking she was supposed to know me. That had been the great, terrible struggle she had been grappling so bravely with. What her session with Mike finally made clear to her was that she didn't know me—didn't have memories of our courtship and marriage—and, more important, wasn't supposed to know me, or be responsible for knowing me, because her memory of the period from about a year and a half before the accident to four months after was erased.

Does this seem extremely confusing? Imagine what it must have been like for Krickitt.

Mike came up with a plan. My relationship with Krickitt, he said, had changed from one of husband and wife—equals—to one of coach/athlete or parent/child—where one of us had all the control and the other was just following orders. We had to reestablish the equality in our marriage that had been swept away by the events of the previous year and a half. We also had to rebuild a shared history.

"You and Krickitt have to have a fresh start," Mike explained. "Krickitt doesn't have any stockpile of shared memories with you. Shared memories leave a trail of emotional attachment that she could trace back to the time you met, reliving all the fellowship and growing and tender moments that lead up to a happy marriage. It's an emotional journey she doesn't remember taking, so it's no wonder she looks around and says, 'How in the world did I get here?'

"A new set of memories that she can remember—that she's a part of—will build new emotional ties between you. I think the old Krickitt is gone. It's time you got to know the new one as well as you knew her."

"So what do we do now?" I asked.

"How did you get to know the old Krickitt?" he came back.

"We went out. Went to ball games, the movies, had dinner with friends . . ."

"Then get to know the new Krickitt the same way."

"Start dating my own wife?" I wondered aloud.

"It's a way to replace the memories Krickitt has lost," he said. "To her, you don't have a past together, nothing to build a marriage relationship on. It's a second chance to court her."

A second chance. Those words sent an unexpected surge of excitement through me. For months I'd felt like I was on the deck of a sinking ship, watching the water get closer and powerless to do anything about it. Mike had just launched my life raft.

Krick and I had nothing to lose. If we were going to fight anyway, we might as well be eating pizza. There wasn't all that much to do in Las Vegas, New Mexico, but I promised her that every week from now on we'd have date night. It wasn't that we did anything earth-shattering; it was that we did it together. We ate pizza (and didn't fight too much). We went bowling. We went to ball games. At Wal-Mart we'd let an employee pick out a bag of candy and share it with them in the store; when we left, Krickitt would pay for the empty bag.

Krickitt appreciated the break in routine, and I liked it too. We got along pretty well on these little excursions, partly because they usually involved eating. Early in her rehab, when there was very little she could enjoy, Krickitt loved food and mealtime. She still did, particularly Snickers bars and the old favorite, frozen yogurt.

One date that turned out to be a true disaster was golf. The first time we played, we didn't make it through the second hole before

Krickitt stomped off in one direction and I stomped off in another. I was trying to be a father again, and she didn't like it. She was tired of me not understanding her and her new personality. With the uninhibited sarcasm of a five-year-old, she let me have it with both barrels.

"I'm sorry," I said in response. "But if you'd quit being such a whiner, you'd do a lot better, and all these people wouldn't be staring at us."

With an icy stare, she threw down her ball and putter and stalked off to the parking lot.

As tough as it was at first, we both decided to give golf another try. It forced us to get along if we wanted to play. The second experience was pretty much a repeat of our first game. Still we tried it another week, forging ahead bravely for two or three holes before we brought the big guns out and aimed them at each other. After a few tries we could make it all the way through the fourth hole before the pyrotechnics began.

There were highs and lows in the dating game with us the same as there are with any couple. The general trend, though, was definitely positive. Our dates gave us something to talk about besides the accident and its consequences. We relaxed more. Laughed more. Looked in each other's eyes more. Kissed more. The momentum had definitely, miraculously, shifted from worse and worse to better and better.

Krickitt, Mike, and I met regularly to talk about our progress. Mike's plan seemed to be working. Krick and I were building a shared past as a foundation for a new future, and our day-to-day relationship was clearly brightening, though we still fought way too much. I hoped the worst was behind us and could imagine us staying together after all, a far cry from where we'd been only a few months before.

Then Mike dropped another bombshell. He wanted us to have a rededication ceremony. That's what he called it, but it sounded a lot like a second wedding to me.

My immediate reaction was, *No way!*

The idea bothered me for several reasons. First of all, we were already married. Would a rededication service mean that we thought our first round of dedication had worn out or dried up? Second, I didn't see any point in going to so much trouble for a purely symbolic gesture. Third, it was yet another big expense at a time when our financial situation was a complete disaster.

Krick was just the opposite. She latched onto the idea as soon as Mike suggested it. I've never known if the two of them cooked this up ahead of time or not, but I was the odd man out from the first.

Krickitt explained her point of view to Mike and me. "I've gotten to know my lifetime buddy again," she said, echoing my words when I proposed to her in California, which seemed like a million years ago. "We've had so much fun. How can you not care deeply for somebody who's stood by you like Kimmer's stood by me? I want to remember giving my hand to him in marriage. Another ceremony will give me the memories every wife should have."

I still had an uneasy feeling about the whole thing, but seeing Krickitt so excited and animated made me think maybe I should do it because it would make her happy. Even if it didn't mean as much to me, the fact was it couldn't hurt.

When she was still an outpatient at Barrow, she had told the therapist there that she missed "that guy" who called her sometimes.

Now she was excited at the idea of having a wedding with "that guy" she could remember.

"I have snapshot memories—flash memories—of my life just before the accident, but I don't have heart memories," she said as we talked with Mike. "That's what I want to get back, something in my heart.

"I want to remember wearing a big, white wedding dress, and having my dad give me away. I want to know what it feels like.

"When I lost my memory, I lost my feelings for Kim. I had to rediscover what it was about Kim I had fallen in love with before. The second time around, my love has grown in a different way—not that 'fluffy' romantic love, but more of a conscious choice. The fact was, I was married to this man. The feelings came later, and by God's grace I've grown to love him again."

That's when I knew I wasn't the only one who had kept a vow. Krickitt kept her vow to honor and support a man she didn't even recognize. For better or worse, as she said with a smile: "I'm stuck with you for life. We *will* make it work. There is no other option."

"You coached me through rehab," she said to me with conviction. "You taught me how to walk again. How to hold a fork. Even helped me go to the bathroom. Now I want you to see me as your wife, not your daughter."

Amen to that.

I decided to restage my marriage proposal by surprising Krickitt at the fitness center where she worked part-time. On Valentine's Day, 1996, I came in with a bouquet of roses, got down on one knee in the employees' office, and, as a small crowd gathered, I slipped her wedding ring off her finger and asked, "Krisxan, will you be my lifetime buddy?"

She said yes, and I slid the ring back onto her finger. But I could tell she was a little disappointed that I wasn't more creative. Looking back on it, I can see she was probably right. Neither the atmosphere nor the aroma of an exercise studio is very conducive to tender romantic moments.

Frankly, I started out doing the whole remarriage thing to make Krickitt happy; but the idea grew on me, and before long I was as excited about another wedding as she was. However, this was not going to be a pull-out-all-the-stops deal like the first ceremony had been. Instead we wanted something quieter and more intimate.

We found a rustic log chapel (so rustic it didn't even have electricity) at Pendaries, a resort in the little town of Sapello, not far from Las Vegas, that was perfect. It only held about thirty people, and since we were only inviting a few close friends, that would be plenty of room.

I waited to propose to Krickitt until the insurance settlement was over because I knew that she wanted to wait until after this was final to have the wedding, and I heartily agreed. No sense in having such a cloud hanging over the festivities. A few weeks later, we got word that everything was in order and paid up—one more reason to celebrate a new beginning.

As the day approached, Krickitt was the picture of confidence, though she warned us the veneer of composure was pretty thin. "I'm going to be a bawling mess when I walk down that aisle," she predicted. "That's when it's going to hit me—everything that's happened in the last two and a half years."

Megan Almquist had been maid of honor at our first wedding and accepted the invitation to do it again. She was looking forward to watching Krickitt make a memory she would hang onto. For best man this time around, the choice had to be Krickitt's favorite physical terrorist, Scott Madsen, who had become such a blessing to us and such an important part of our lives. His encouragement during some of my darkest days had been an incredible gift.

The night before the ceremony, Krickitt stayed with her family at their hotel and I stayed at our apartment. She was in a room with her friends from California when Jamey (who'd come to perform the ceremony) ran wide-eyed into the room.

"Jay Leno's talking about you guys!"

The girls all ran to the TV in the next room. Sure enough, mention of our courting and marrying a second time had made it onto the *Tonight* show. As Krickitt would say, wow.

Some very special people came to share our new beginning with us. We saw many of the nurses, doctors, and therapists who had been God's instruments for saving Krickitt's life. DJ Coombs—the EMT who'd overcome her claustrophobia to treat Krick when she was still hanging upside down in the car—was there; as was Bob Grothe, the flight nurse on the helicopter from Gallup to Albuquerque when Krick so nearly left us; and Wayne and Kelli Marshall, the couple who had stopped at the scene of the accident and prayed for us.

As we had done before, Krickitt and I wrote our vows. On May 25, 1996, I stood in the front of the little mountain chapel at Pendaries, faced the great love of my life in the presence of God and that small body of witnesses, and spoke with an assurance and love and deepest thanksgiving that I will never be able to describe. I saw the tears in Krisxan's eyes sparkling through the tears in my own.

"Krick, I stand before you once again, reaffirming the commitment of vows I once made. I thank God every day for sparing our lives and providing strength and will to endure these trials and tribulations. Two and one-half years ago I made a vow before God. And as I stated then and state now with greater love and desire:

"I promise to defend our love and hold it in highest regard. I promise to be forgiving, understanding, and patient. I promise to tend to your every need. I promise to respect and honor you fully.

"Most of all, I promise that no matter the adversaries we may face I will never ever lose the vow of commitment to protect you, guide you, and care for you until death do us part.

"Only one thing can surpass forever the painful events that we have felt. That is the love I have for you, and I thank the Lord for his guidance and faith in me to love you. I am truly honored to be your husband."

Krickitt's vows were a lot shorter. But she said it all.

"Kimmer, I love you. I cherish you as my husband. Thank you for being true to your first vows. I promise to be here for you, to encourage you and comfort you in your time of need. I pray that I may be the wife that the Lord desires for you to have.

"I need you Kimmer. And I love you."

I took out her old wedding ring (no baseballs this time) to give her again. Krickitt was wearing the same gown she'd worn to our first wedding, and we'd agreed to use the same rings. Without telling her, I had also bought a new ring and planned to put them both on her finger together when the time came.

After I slipped them on her finger side by side, Megan handed Krickitt my old ring to give to me. With it in the palm of her hand was a new second ring, gold with the Christian icthus symbol representing all the Lord had done in our lives. I wasn't the only one who could stage a last-minute surprise! As she slipped the two rings on where the old one had been, a long-absent thousand-megawatt smile filled my field of vision. And my heart.

For our honeymoon, I took Krickitt back to the same hotel on Maui we'd gone to after our first wedding. Driving to the beach we saw a sign that read, "Jesus Is Coming Soon." Krickitt had a flash memory of it but no context to put it in. I took her to a place that had been our favorite spot on the beach on our first trip.

"Something clicks," she said, looking at a patio with some tables and chairs scattered across it. She even showed me the table we sat at in '93. "But it's deja vu minus me."

That was the last time we tried to jog her memory. From that moment on we gave it up to God. Our lives were in his hands, and he was having us look to the future, not to the past.

And our future, it turned out, was being rewritten at that very moment in ways we never could have imagined.

Chapter 11

MAJOR MOMENTUM

*T*here were a lot of similarities between our two weddings: same dress, same rings, same maid of honor, same honeymoon trip. And then there were the differences the second time around: CBS Television, the London *Times*, and *Inside Edition*. Between my proposal to Krickitt on Valentine's Day 1996 and our ceremony May 25, we got a crash course in media relations.

It started with a prayer Krickitt prayed. People who heard our story seemed encouraged by it, so one day she prayed that the Lord would use our story for his own glory. "I put it in God's hands," she told me, "and if anything happens with it, it will be only because of him."

Days later, we got a call out of the blue from Van Tate, host of a TV show called *On the Road* on the Albuquerque CBS affiliate. Van heard about our accident and plans to have a second wedding ceremony. He wanted to do a segment of the show on us. Of course we were jazzed at all the attention, even though we didn't feel like we deserved any special recognition. All we were doing was living out the vows we had made to each other and giving glory to God that we'd been able to do that.

Van did a nice piece about us, and a day or two later a reporter from the *Albuquerque Journal* called and wanted to do a story too. And so on Sunday, March 17, 1996, we were front-page news in Albuquerque under the headline "Love Lost & Refound." The article went into more detail about our accident and Krickitt's rehab. Again the angle was that after all that had happened we were not only still married but were going to renew our wedding vows.

Krick and I were both happy that the article didn't shy away from the importance of faith in our lives. On the second page of the story there was a big photo of the two of us praying in front of an open Bible.

I also liked the quote they put in near the end: "I'm not marrying the same person I married three years ago, but I'm not the same person either. For instance, baseball doesn't mean what it used to mean to me. That was part of our old life. We're closer now; we've got a different bond, a more meaningful connection than before. My friends say I've become a religious freak. No, I tell them, I've just seen the miracles that God's work can provide."

Up to that time we had never thought of it as anything special—we hadn't seen our situation as something that ought to be on the evening news. But the media looked at it a different way. The moment of truth came when we got a call from Tom Colbert, president of a company called Industry Research and Development that looks for human interest stories in the news and helps local reporters connect with national media. He saw the article in the paper and asked us if we wanted him to release our story through the Associated Press. He explained that once it was fed to the AP network, it would be available to hundreds of newspapers and other news outlets across the country.

"You need to think carefully about this," he advised us. "Because if we do this, your lives are never going to be the same."

He made it sound like a scary proposition. But hadn't it been only a week ago that we were saying, "Lord, we have this great story. How can we use it to glorify you?" After we thought and prayed hard about it, we felt at peace with the idea and said yes. We didn't think much would happen anyway, since by this time the wreck had happened almost two and a half years ago.

Tom knew what he was talking about. As soon as our story broke nationally, the momentum started picking up in a major way. Every day we got more calls than the day before, until the phone would ring again as soon as we put it down. The day before our wedding there was a feature article in the *Los Angeles Times*. That article and the Associated Press story generated more than two hundred telephone calls to our house. Newspaper columnists, TV reporters, producers for talk shows, magazine writers, and everybody else who had anything to do with news called practically nonstop. It was unmistakably the work of the Lord.

We talked to as many media people as we could, but it was obvious that we had to make some kind of order out of all this chaos. *Inside Edition* asked us for exclusive rights to cover our wedding in exchange for paying for the wedding and our honeymoon. We felt this was the Lord taking control, opening the door for us to give the glory to him.

Also, a free wedding was not a bad thing.

During the days leading up to the ceremony, we spent some time with *Inside Edition* telling our story and giving them background material. They ran their first feature on us a couple of weeks before the wedding. Though I had sort of been in the public eye as a college coach, being interviewed for a national TV show was a new experience. The reporter and crew came to our house in Las Vegas and set up their lights and other gear in the living room. They shot us watching the video of our first wedding and Krickitt looking at pictures and other mementos of a day she no longer remembered.

We also gave an advance interview to *Day and Date*, though because of our agreement with *Inside Edition* they weren't able to tape during the ceremony. (They did, however, shanghai the bridesmaids outside after the ceremony and interview them then.)

There wasn't a bride's room in the little log church at Pendaries, so we had Krickitt's parents' RV parked out in front for Krickitt to use as a dressing room. True to their name, *Inside Edition* was inside with her, squeezed in with bridesmaids and everybody else, talking to Krick about her dress, how she felt, and all that other bride-before-the-wedding stuff.

Though *Inside Edition* was on the inside, there were plenty of other people waiting on the outside. There was a photographer from the London *Times* and another from *People* magazine. Supposedly no one in the media knew where we were going on our honeymoon, but there was a rumor that *Hard Copy* learned we were going to Hawaii and said they'd have a crew waiting for us at the airport in Honolulu. That was too much. Krick and I were eager to share our story but not eager to share our honeymoon with a TV news show. I called the airport police in Honolulu and explained the situation. But we never saw a trace of them.

We did, however, get a call for a telephone interview a day or two after we arrived. A reporter for a radio show called us live from

California at 4 A.M. Hawaii time. The hotel had generally been great about keeping our presence a secret. If people called, they said there was no Mr. & Mrs. Kim J. Carpenter registered there (which was true—we registered under aliases). But there was a new guy at the switchboard who wasn't in the loop. The radio station was calling every hotel on Maui trying to smoke us out. They had called all but two when they got to ours, then the operator put him through. I never heard that interview (I'm not even sure who it was for), but I bet it wasn't one of our best.

The first *Inside Edition* story ran before our wedding. The second one ran while we were in Hawaii. That same week *Day and Date* ran its story, illustrated with home video footage since our deal with *Inside Edition* meant they couldn't tape the ceremony. People started recognizing us on the street in Maui. "Hey, didn't I see you guys on TV yesterday?" Our anonymity was crumbling fast.

At the end of the week we arrived back at the L.A. airport. We were blown away to see our faces in *Star* magazine. Immediately we knew who had reported the story and taken the pictures for them. There had been one particularly obnoxious stranger hovering around the front of the church during the ceremony, getting in front of our family video camera and in front of *Inside Edition*'s. We had tried to keep a wary eye on him and told one of the ushers to show him the door if he kept being obnoxious, but there was too much going on to worry about him. Thus, we were now stars of the supermarket tabloids.

As soon as we got back to Las Vegas, we were flooded with requests and invitations from syndicated TV shows. We wanted to accept as many as we could and ended up sometimes being in two or three different places in the same week. We did some regional shows like *Northwest Afternoon* in Seattle, but most of the shows we traveled to be on were national. (Even in Seattle people recognized us. By that time we'd been on TV in Japan, and a bunch of Japanese tourists practically mobbed us outside the studio.)

Through it all, our friend and neighbors in New Mexico were great. To them we were the same old Kim and Krickitt. They were the same friendly, supportive people they'd always been, and never made a big deal about any of the fuss.

For the first shows we did, crews came to interview us in New Mexico. It wasn't long before we got invitations to New York and L.A. to be interviewed in person by the hosts. Except for Krickitt's mission trip to Hungary, neither of us had traveled much. The talk-show circuit was a whole new experience. I don't have any interest in changing careers, but show business types sure do know how to impress a couple of people from New Mexico.

We were taken to the best restaurants, cruised around town in our own chauffeured limousine, and generally felt like celebrities for a day or two. (We always got a chuckle out of the star treatment. Krickitt said it made up for all the homecoming and prom night limo rides she never got.) The super thing about it, though, is that having a taste of show business was a great way to reaffirm what's truly important in life. For all the attention we started getting, we were the same people after we went on TV as we were before. Still two people trying to work out our lives together, glorify God in our relationship, and keep our promises to each other.

Being with celebrities gave us the unexpected opportunity to share with them on a personal level and get to know them as something besides talking heads. Sally Jesse Raphael's producers asked us to appear on her show because Sally has a son with a head injury caused by a motorcycle crash, and she saw our story as a way to educate the public on the devastating effect of injuries like that. As tragic as it was, her experience gave us a shared understanding of what a life-changing event such an injury can be. She could talk to us because she knew that we knew firsthand what she was going through. I also think her son's experience helped her interview us with extra insight and sensitivity.

We were on *Leeza* and found Leeza Gibbons was truly an elegant and classy lady. We enjoyed meeting Anne Curry on *Dateline* and also had fun with Maury Povich on his program. While we were in New York to do his show, we saw people playing games around little tables set up on the sidewalk. I thought that was kind of cool and decided to join in the fun. Just as I put some money down on the table somebody yelled, "Cops!" In a heartbeat the other player scooped the money off the table and hightailed it down the street.

He stole my money! I took off chasing him and so did another player. In the excitement I left Krick behind with her parents. When I didn't come back, she stopped a police car and asked the officer to look for me. He asked her what I looked like. She started to describe me, then stopped and held up a copy of the newest issue of *People* magazine, which we had just bought at a newsstand. She flipped to the story in it about our wedding and said, "That's him!" It was a four-page feature called "Married to a Stranger," and the issue even had a picture of Krick and my dad making a face on the contents page.

The police officers went cruising for me but didn't see me. When Krick finally went back to our hotel, I was already there. I never got my money back. In fact, I had given twenty bucks to the other guy who was chasing that shyster with me because he didn't have any more money for a cab home.

Some of the best trips of all were to Nashville and Los Angeles for the *Crook & Chase* show. Lori Ann Crook and Charlie Chase were a blast. We also got a call to be on *Oprah*, which is consistently one of the highest rated shows on the tube. She gave us the opportunity to share our faith with her audience and made it possible for us to reach more people at once than we ever had before.

Before the year was out, we also had major stories in *McCall's* ("The Wife Who Forgot She Was Married") and *Reader's Digest* ("For Better, For Worse"). The *Digest* article, in the December 1996 issue, had a great quote from Krickitt explaining why she was looking forward to our second wedding: "People think we're getting married a second time to make my memory come back. But I have accepted the fact that part of my life is erased." She wasn't looking to the past, but to the future. "Every woman should have that moment to remember." Thank God this one did.

We also got wonderful support from the Christian media. *New Man* magazine featured us in their first issue of 1997. We were both especially grateful for the message James Dobson put in his "Family News" letter that following June. He reprinted the story about us from *Reader's Digest*, then summed up in a way that made us feel so humble and so blessed to be instruments of God's teaching to others:

> In this day when the culture teaches us to bail out at
> the first sign of frustration or pain, it is uplifting to see
> this young couple work to recapture what they had lost
> and to remain committed to each other even in the face
> of tragedy. Their example will, I hope, be relevant to
> many of my readers who have lost the passion in their
> marriages—not as a result of brain injury, but from
> whatever has driven them apart. Perhaps Kim's decision
> to win Krickitt's affection anew will be especially helpful

to those who have misplaced the "memory" of love. If you have been considering a divorce, wouldn't it be better to begin courting your spouse again and seeking to rebuild the marriage from the ground up? That is never easy and I'm sure Kim and Krickitt have not yet faced their final challenges. But it is the right thing to do, and ultimately, the most rewarding response for disengaging husbands and wives. And it is *definitely* in the best interests of children.

Let me conclude by offering a word of advice to young men and women who will be joining hands in holy matrimony during this summer. . . . I urge each of you to enter into marriage with an unshakable commitment to make it last a lifetime. Let nothing short of death separate what is about to be consummated. When the hard times come (and they WILL come), I hope you will remember the story of Kim and Krickitt who are weathering the storm together—hand in hand and soul to soul. That is God's plan for the family—and for *your* family.

Christian Reader put us on the cover of their November/ December 1997 issue and titled their story "Loving a Perfect Stranger." Our second wedding was a year and a half in the past by then, but by the miraculous providence of God, we were still big news. When our story came out in the *Los Angeles Times* and *Inside Edition,* a lot of people in the media business told us to take advantage of every opportunity to tell our story because soon we'd be old news and nobody would want to book us.

It didn't turn out that way at all. We never solicited appearances or interviews, but the media kept calling. They couldn't seem to get enough of the story, and we were happy to go anywhere, anytime to tell it. The publicity also brought a huge demand for Krickitt and me to speak in churches, marriage enrichment groups, and to all sorts of other audiences. Neither one of us had much experience at it. Still, we were willing to do it for the sake of sharing God's gift to us, and somehow he put the right words in our mouths. He answered our prayers and kept the story alive for his glory.

It's ironic that Krickitt is so clearly the focus of many of the stories. She's the one who has suffered and had her life so fundamentally changed. She's been through a miraculous process of healing and recovery that people are naturally interested in and curious about. Yet everything she knows about those events is something somebody else told her.

Interviewers will ask, "How did you feel hanging upside down in the car?" or "What was it like waking up in the hospital?" or "What was it like to walk again after the doctors said you never would?" And Krickitt will patiently answer, "I don't remember any of that. What they tell me is . . ." She is the leading figure in a drama she will never remember. Due to her retrograde amnesia, those memories are gone for good.

I think that's a blessing because since she did go through it, people take her testimony seriously. But since she doesn't remember it, she has been providentially spared the nightmares and pain those memories would surely kindle. We've had a second chance few people in the world have had.

In the midst of all the media interest, Hollywood came calling. Tom Colbert, who had helped us from the very first with media relations, stepped in to guide us through the motion-picture industry maze. Several studios wanted to take an option on our story. We found out that meant they were interested in doing a feature film (or in some cases a made-for-TV special), and would pay a nonrefundable holding fee to have exclusive film rights to our story for a certain period. At the end of the period, they could renew their option, or let it go, in which case we could make a deal with somebody else.

After a lot of prayer, we made a decision to go with Paul Taublieb and his LXD Productions. Of everyone we talked to, Paul had the best understanding of what we've been through, and what we want a movie about us to accomplish. He ultimately got us to Caravan Pictures and to Roger Birnbaum, who made the hit movie *While You Were Sleeping*. The film project is now continuing in development with Spyglass Entertainment, a new production company associated with Walt Disney Pictures.

There's bound to be some Hollywood plot enhancements and re-arrangement of the story to put four years' worth of stuff into a two-hour screenplay. What we want people to see on the screen most of all is the way God worked in our lives, saved Krickitt from almost certain death, and built an awesome new marriage for us on the twisted foundation of the old one.

I like the way Paul described his take on our story. He said, "It's unique because it's a romance that takes place within a marriage. These days, people look at each other wrong over breakfast and get a divorce." Divorce is breaking your promise to God, and there's no excuse for it, even though most of the world doesn't see it that way anymore. We want this movie to lift up solid, spiritually-based values in a world that's desperate for them. There's a God-shaped hole in everyone that only God can fill. Without God, every marriage is at risk. With God, every marriage is safe and unassailable. Not always sweetness and light but always safe and unassailable.

I think what has kept our story alive all this time is that it is a story of hope. Hope is in short supply in the world these days. It would have been so easy for either of us to give up during the long and sometimes dark years since the accident. I can't help thinking about the story of Job that Krick and I read the first time we visited each other. There have been many times when I identified completely with this poor servant of God, who went from a life of plenty and happiness to the pit of despair. Yet God brought him through the refiner's fire and eventually heaped riches on him far greater than what he had lost.

> The LORD blessed the latter part of Job's life more than the first. He had fourteen thousand sheep, six thousand camels, a thousand yoke of oxen and a thousand donkeys. And he also had seven sons and three daughters. . . . Nowhere in all the land were there found women as beautiful as Job's daughters, and their father granted them an inheritance along with their brothers. . . .
> And so he died, old and full of years.
> (Job 42:12–13, 15, 17, NIV)

I don't think I could hold up under what Job had to endure. But I think I have some sense of what he went through. And my life is no less a miracle than his was. No less an awesome and unbelievable gift.

Chapter 12

KRICKITT'S DIARY 4—
"May your light shine on me"

5/24/96

Lord,

Thank you for this time to sit at your feet and relax. It is kind of stressful doing all of the last-minute things for my wedding, only because I want our day tomorrow to be special. It feels nice to relax and think about life & you. Please Lord, I pray for a gorgeous day tomorrow, and I pray that it won't rain. Allow everyone's journey up to Pendaries to be nice and comforting. I pray for all of the details of the wedding to flow well. I know that you are in control. Please allow the wind to be mellow tomorrow. May everyone get to and from the airport safely and have safe plane flights.

I pray that the media will be polite and respectful. Please allow them to see the awesome things you have done in our lives.

I pray for everyone in the wedding, that they may be organized and mindful of all that is going on. Please open my mind and heart to say the words in my vows you wish. May you please fill Jamey with your Spirit to say what you desire for him to say.

I pray for K&I that we may spend some quality times together sharing, laughing, & caring. I pray for our second honeymoon, that it may really go well. I can't wait. I need your strength, Lord, and your Spirit, Please help me & Kimmer to grow closer together. Open my mind & heart to say your words. I love you.

—Kricky

8/3

1 Cor 10:13 "No temptation has overtaken you except what is common to man; and God is faithful, who will not allow you to be tempted beyond what you are able, but with the temptation will provide

the way of escape also, that you may be able to endure it."

These words I wrote on the airplane flying to
Nashville—I was really sad and Kimmer and I had
just had an argument on the way to the airport.

Jesus, I need you to keep sane. I desire someone
so bad that I can really talk to. I know you are always there.

I am trying to seek you, Lord. You are the true
one who understands and cares. I need you. I love
you, Jesus.

—KC

8/19/96

Today Lord, I come to you thankful that my
walk with you is growing a lot. I thank you for the
sweet times of fellowship I have had with you in the
AMs. It is my prayer that I will continue to walk
with you and seek you daily at the start of my day.
I love you—Krick

I pray for <u>Megan</u> and <u>Lisa</u>; for <u>Kim</u>—job, health,
communication, Disney contract, book deal; for me:

9/4/96

Lord–

I pray that you would truly lift me up today. I feel as though my heart was really heavy when I went to sleep last night. I'm sure I'm fighting some depression, but I pray that you would give me the true joy that comes from you. I know I can stand tall with you.

I pray that your Holy Spirit may fill me today and allow your light to shine.

I pray that you would fill me and help me with my patience. Help me as I go back to work today. I pray that you would help me not to complain, worry, gripe, etc. I place these downfalls of my per-sonality and drastic changes in your hands. I truly need your help, Lord.

I pray for Kim and me that your Spirit would draw us closer to you, which will draw us closer to-gether. I pray for my walk. Please draw me closer to you. Please show K how to walk daily. I pray and desire a spiritual leader so badly. I pray that he may be the man you so desire.

Please walk with us today. I love you. —KC

10/11/96

Lord,

I cry out to you for your help. I know that you are there for me.

I need you. I feel really stripped of my joy these days. I ask that you fill me with your Holy Spirit and build me up according to your desires. I need you and your Spirit to guide me.

I pray for K&I. We have no quality time with you together. I pray that you would work on Kim's heart and show him where & how he needs to be my spiritual leader. Please open our eyes and show us truth.

I pray that _you_ would be the one to lift Kim out of his depression and give him _guidance_ and direction. Show us your will. We love you. I love you.

—Krick

Dec 17 '96

Lord,

I love you and know that you are here for me. I pray that you will hear my concerns on _what_ I need to do to be a better wife for you. I pray that

your will will be done with Kimmer and me even
though that scares me at times, but I trust you.

[diaries for 1997 and the first nine months of 1998 are missing]

9/30/98
Lord Jesus,
Thank you for who you are. I love you & need
you so bad. I pray for you to take over my body &
make me more like you. I feel so jumpy & moody,
but I trust you, God, to help me through this hard
time.

I feel alone here in Farmington, but it is getting
better. I pray that I may feel you & see you more. I
thank you for all that you are doing. I have really
seen you work over the past months & I thank you
for that. May you shine through me so powerfully
today. Strengthen my mind and allow it to remain
tough & continue to get better. I trust you & know
you have been and are working. I ask in faith that
you continue to deliver me.

Lord God, I pray that our <u>*house*</u> *in* <u>*Vegas*</u> *will*
sell soon. Please Lord. You know our financial

situation, and I pray that you will help us &
allow us to get a good contract that goes through.

I pray for a job for me. I have fears of not enough
work. Please guide me & provide some work for me.
I know you have the job in mind. May I grow in
that and know you are in control.

May you grow in me & help me not to be tempted
by wacky thoughts. I give them over to you—I don't understand them, and I pray for your growth & strength
to shine through.

May you help me to grow as a child & help me
to share <u>your joy, your love</u>, & your grace & forgiveness. I love You & need you. Help K & I to grow.
—KC

10/7/98
Lord,

I pray that you, God, would forgive me for being
selfish, for bitterness and my fears & unworthiness.
You know exactly where I am right now. May you
please wrap your loving arms around me & extend
your grace to me. May I have a peace in my mind
& spirit & may you guard my heart & mind in

Christ Jesus. I know you are faithful & you have brought me out of these mind struggles before—I pray to see your power on this day.

I pray for a job for me. Put me where you want me. You know our finances. May you be glorified. May my eyes be fixed & focused on you, God. May Kimmer & I grow more each minute in our love for each other. May you help me to serve my husband unselfishly. You know my heart & I pray for your strength. Be my strength. May my eyes be on you.

God, may you see me through this move to Farmington that is hard. Please be my comfort & my strength. I need you, Lord. Be my strength & my focus. —Krickitt

10/11/98

Please guide me with Kimmer. Please take control & show me how I can communicate with him. I ask God that you would speak to him.

Glory be to you—that Kim & I can be alive together to sharpen one another. Build me strong & strengthen me with the power of your Holy Spirit. Lift up my heart. Joy to fill me. —KC

10/23/98

As my mind has continued to race for months, oh how I pray for deliverance from this racing. I don't understand it, Lord, but I am going to trust you in this one. Running & racing in circles, I don't get why it has been so crazy. Peace, peace, peace of mind is what I pray for. I pray for a release of the racing, a deliverance of the dwelling on the crazy stuff. May you give me a peace of mind like I haven't experienced in years. You say ask & you shall receive. Ask I do. I believe your Word and ask for deliverance from the mind games. May I turn it all over to you right now, knowing that I have <u>victory</u> in you. Help me please to program my mind on you, Lord. May my eyes be <u>fixed</u> on you. May my heart's desire be to serve you more. May my love, attraction, excitement, & desire grow more & more, deeper & deeper, richer & richer in depth with my Kimmer each day. Each minute.

May you clear up my head & my mind. I pray for freedom in Christ, free to live. May you further develop confidence in me. May you guide Kimmer & me in our ministry. I thank you for Kim & his *commitment to me. I pray for a deepening in our relationship. May you bind us closer.*

Please help me to apply this verse in my life:

"Be anxious for nothing, but in everything by prayer and supplication with thanksgiving let your requests be made known to God.

And the peace of God, which surpasses all comprehension, shall guard your hearts and your minds in Christ Jesus.

Finally, brethren, whatever is true, whatever is honorable, whatever is right, whatever is pure, whatever is lovely, whatever is of good repute, if there is any excellence and if anything worthy of praise, <u>dwell on these things</u>." —Phil. 4:6–8

12/7/98

Lord God,

What a great husband you have given me. He has such a great heart. Thank you for opening his eyes & heart to these kids we heard about on the radio who need things. Please may we be able to help out these children who won't have a Christmas. May they hear the gospel through our efforts. Help make Kimmer & me more like you. Please get my eyes off of myself. I feel like I am doing better with my struggles, only because of you. Please work through us. I pray you'll strengthen our marriage right now.

Lord I pray for Kim & me. I thank you for our intimate time together. May we grow more & more in love this Christmas season. May all other things I am struggling with pass. I lay it at your feet and thank you for our time together. May we grow closer to you, Lord. I love you & need you. Please be my stronghold & rescuer on this day. Be my strength.

—Krickitt

1/4/99

Lord God,

As I start this new year at your feet, may you take control of my body, mind, & soul and make me clean. Even though I fear at times what you may take me through, I trust you. I give you all of me and beg of your mercy & grace on this day. May you restore the excitement in me, in my marriage, and my daily life.

I lay my struggles at your feet & also my mind that has me in such turmoil and confusion. Please clean me and make me new again, fresh, holy & pure before you on this day. If Kim & I need to talk, I put that in your hands. The battles & struggles that lay within me, please burn them to the ground on this day. Make me anew. May I see the growth once again in my life as I seek your face.

I pray that Kim and I would desire each other more & more on this day. I love you and pray for a new start on this new year. Restore unto me the joy of my salvation. Use me, Lord—show me what you want me to do

—Krisxan

1/6/99

Lord,

I give you me on this day. Please make me as pretty on the inside as I feel I once was. I recall the joy, confidence, & excitement for you. Please strengthen my mind & body & spirit/soul today. I need you. I can do nothing without you. God, you are my God. Please take over my mind. Help this

struggle to pass, so I can truly experience <u>true</u> grace
& freedom in Christ. As I draw near to you, may
you draw near to me, as your Word says. Help my
quiet times to provide growth to me. I need you &
pray for a clear & clean mind. May your helmet of
salvation cover me & block all things out that are
not from You. You are an awesome God. I lay my
problems & struggles at your feet. May Kim & I
grow closer together—become more intimate, and
may we experience the true binding process. Help
us to respect one another. We love you & need you,
God.

   —KC

1/10/99
Lord God,
   I thank you for who you are. I praise you & only
you on this day. I give you all of my problems,
struggles, concerns, fears, crazies, & doubts. Please
protect me with your upright hand. May I have the
helmet of salvation on this day. I ask that you clothe
me & cover me on this day. You are so awesome,
holy, & mighty.

I have seen different phases in my life with my head injury—I know in your perfect timing this too will pass. I praise You as I throw it in your hands.

"Therefore, since we have so great a cloud of witnesses surrounding us, let us also lay aside every encumbrance, and the sin which so easily entangles us, and let us run with endurance the race that is set before us, fixing our eyes on Jesus, the author and perfecter of faith, who for the joy set before Him endured the cross, despising the shame, and has sat down at the right hand of the throne of God.

"For consider Him who has endured such hostility by sinners against Himself, so that you may not grow weary and lose heart." —Heb. 12:1–3

Lord that is my heart's cry—be my strength & help me to run with endurance—knowing that you are in control. Make me strong, a fighter. As your sun comes up this morning, may your light shine on me. Be my Lord.

I love you.

I am growing stronger.

Please help me to press on.

Chapter 13

A VICTORY OF FAITH

*I*n the summer of 1998, we moved back to my hometown of Farmington in northwestern New Mexico near the Four Corners. There were TV reporters at our house before we got the boxes unpacked. Before the week was out, our picture was splashed across the local news section of the Farmington *Daily Times* with a headline reading "Carpenters Keeping 'The Vow': Famous couple moves to town as world watches," and a sidebar that said "*Dateline* to feature couple on Monday."

We visited several local churches before deciding the Lord was leading us to worship at Piñon Hills Community Church. They stood out right away because they were so sincerely supportive and friendly. They made us feel at home.

The media invitations kept coming, and we kept accepting them. Not only were viewers not tired of our story; they wanted more. At least one show saved their interview with us to run during rating sweeps week, when the networks measure their viewing audience to set advertising rates. We were on TV in Germany, and in Japan we were featured on a show titled *The World's Top Ten Stories.*

One experience we had that we'll never forget was when a scruffy looking biker dude came up to us at the airport. We both tensed up because he was so intimidating, and I was already mentally resigned to handing over my wallet.

At that moment the guy said, "I just want to tell you, man, that your story is really cool. Really cool." He shook our hands, we talked for a minute, and then he walked off. As we raced to catch our plane, we decided that God's people come in all shapes, sizes—and fashion trends.

In Farmington I became chief administrator of a partnership program between New Mexico Highlands University and the local San Juan Community College that allowed Farmington residents to take Highlands extension courses. Krickitt began a part-time job as a lead fitness aide at San Juan College's Fitness Center, which was open to the community. After a few months she decided to make a change and take on a bigger challenge. She began substitute teaching at Kirtland Central High School, and it ended up being almost a full-time job. She called herself The Mean Sub because, unlike some substitutes, she made her students toe the line in discipline and getting their work done. No slacking off just because the regular teacher was absent.

Of course the students knew about her story, and sometimes they asked her to share it with them. "If you're good, I'll tell you," she would promise. She had many, many opportunities to share her testimony at Kirtland. And having a different class to teach almost every day was challenging and good for her recovery. She greatly appreciates her time at KCHS and misses the students much—GO BRONCOS!

After school was out that summer, Krickitt started to volunteer at San Juan Regional Medical Center in their cardiopulmonary rehab department. Although she was used to exercising generally healthy individuals in Las Vegas, she really enjoyed the challenge of working with the patients who were starting an exercise program in SJRMC's Cardiac and Pulmonary Rehab. After about a month of volunteering, the hospital hired her on as staff to assist in the growing rehab program. Today she is in the cardiopulmonary department at SJRMC, working with "her kids," who range up to eighty years in age.

We've been able to pay back every penny we ever owed, and now by God's grace we can give something to others in need. The Christmas after we moved to Farmington, a radio station made an appeal for toys to give as gifts to children who wouldn't have any Christmas presents otherwise. They asked listeners to bring a toy or two for one child. We decided to take them up on it. We took our SUV to the toy store and filled it up, then drove over to the station to drop everything off.

I walked inside to the front desk and told the receptionist we had some toys to contribute and needed help unloading them. She said, "Just put them in that box over there."

"You don't understand," I said. "We've got a lot. I mean a whole lot."

She followed me to the door, took a look at the car and let out a gasp.

"Just a minute and I'll get somebody," she said finally.

Help arrived, and a minute later we unloaded enough toys for more than forty children. We plan to help others every year. It isn't our money anyway; it's God's.

Of all the opportunities we've had since our second wedding, the best part is what an incredible witness opportunity the Lord has given us. We had a horrible experience, a three-year nightmare. In the middle of it all, it was impossible to imagine anything good ever could have come out of it. Yet God in his wisdom has lifted up hundreds of opportunities to share our story and our faith. A publicist once told me we've been seen or heard by an estimated six hundred million people around the world. That's twice the population of the United States.

A lot of the speaking we do is at church services or parachurch events. I think there's something in our story for everyone, but we try to make one point very clear, very early in our presentations whether they're in church or on network TV: we don't have a story without the Lord. The great victory in our marriage isn't us; it's faith.

We've had the opportunity to share our lives on *The 700 Club* with Pat Robertson, and have been featured in *Focus on the Family*. Those are places where our audiences, I think, have a special understanding of the faith aspect of our story. It's only by God's grace that Krickitt is still with me today and that together we can share our experiences. It's about a commitment to God and a commitment to each other. We were helpless, the doctors were helpless, the best medical technology was helpless. God came through with his abundant blessings just like the Book of Job promises.

We also share what we know about the power of praying for specifics. God can do anything, and you shouldn't be afraid to ask for a very specific blessing. Right after the accident, we prayed for the pressure on Krickitt's brain to go down. It went down in minutes, even though the doctors told us it wasn't going to go down fast enough, and if she lived, she'd be a vegetable. The same thing happened later in the day with her blood pressure. We prayed for it to go up, and it did. This doesn't mean you should expect any prayer to be answered so quickly and obviously—we can't know God's perfect will. But it's an unmistakable example of God's power to answer our heart cry.

Another point we bring up, especially to young audiences, is the wonderful blessing of intimacy in marriage, and the value of saving yourself for your spouse. It's not only God's plan; it's a way of showing your spouse he or she means more to you than anybody else you've ever met. You've saved the ultimate physical relationship for one person alone—the one God has picked just for you. Before we were married, all we did was kiss. Unfortunately, that puts us in a tiny minority these days, since only about 15 percent of women and 10 percent of men are virgins on their wedding day. But there's a power and assurance and satisfaction about sharing the most intimate part of your life with only one person that helps make marriage stronger and more special than it can possibly be otherwise.

There are things that will always be different for us. The Krickitt I'm married to now is not the same person I married in 1993. Her personality has changed 30 to 40 percent. She's less patient, less inhibited, and has a lower frustration threshold. She has to get ten hours of sleep without fail. She gets tired easily and has a harder time concentrating than she did before the injury.

Despite those challenges, she's working now and loves her job. Not long ago we thought she'd never be able to work again, yet here she is, doing what she truly enjoys and has a gift for. No one meeting her today has any idea she ever had a severe head injury, unless they know our history. And she's continuing to improve even after all this time, with no plateau in sight. She forgets things, yes, but she is a fulfilled, happy, productive person. And we have a marriage that God has carried through the refiner's fire.

If she's different, I'm different too. I don't have the narrow focus on my job and my sports career I used to. (I also have to have continuing therapy with my back—heat, analgesics, and exercise.) I'm executive producer of the *Game of the Week* on Christian radio station KNMI, 88.9 FM, in Farmington, so I still have a chance to keep up with the teams, but it isn't life or death any more. I know what life or death is, and baseball isn't it.

I wouldn't have thought it was possible, but I love Krickitt more today than I did the day we got engaged, more than our first wedding day. She has a fantastic curiosity and innocence wrapped in a fun, kind-of-wild personality. I can hardly imagine what faith it took for her finally to believe it when everybody kept telling her she was married to me. "God wanted me to be married to this person," she said. "Everybody said I was, and one day, looking in the mirror, I was convicted by the Lord that it was the truth.

"I trusted God when I married him, so I knew I'd get to know this guy that I married. I don't look back at what is lost. The media does, but I don't live like that. I fix my eyes above."

We've been given a second chance at life together, and neither one of us will ever take each other or our marriage for granted. Every day we have something to be thankful for—like blue eyes, for instance. Krickitt has the most beautiful blue eyes I've ever seen. I get a flutter in my stomach when I look into her eyes.

The media is still interested in us, though I think part of it is watching and waiting to see if we're eventually going to get to each other and split up after all. They've got a long wait ahead of them. Like forever.

We talk about what we learned through years of trial and heartache: courting your spouse all over again will solve all kinds of problems and mend so many marriages. Remember what it was that brought you together in the first place? The shared interests, the shared experiences? Once you stop having those, your marriage will get stale. As the memory of those times gets fainter, you may start wondering what you saw in your spouse in the first place.

You start to drift apart, and before you know it you're at each other's throats over the slightest thing. You look for ways to avoid being together, and once the momentum gets going, it's easy to let it keep on pulling you apart.

But what are the real problems? Money? Boredom? Is one of you ignoring the other? Whatever it is, you can thank God that at least your wife knows who you are. Divorce has become too easy. When you get married, you make a lifetime commitment. You make a promise before God. You need to think about that before you pull the plug. Make a promise to each other that you will never use the D-word.

In all this we're not interested in the attention except as a tool for reaching people with the message *that there is hope and healing for even the most desperately unhappy marriage.* Our message is that what you have to focus on is keeping your promise to God and each other, and sharing the foundation of your strength—faith in him.

We had two weddings and two wedding rings. We also celebrate two wedding anniversaries every year. In very real ways, they both mark new beginnings for us. We don't dwell on the bad times but look ahead to a new life together. Krickitt will never have a memory of falling in love or of our courtship and marriage. But she says that what she felt as a bride the second time was a deeper love than most wives experience in a lifetime. Our life has given us a bond few people will ever be able to understand.

I'm no hero. I'm a sinner saved like anybody can be. I'm still learning patience with a wife who is a different person from the one I married. But none of that matters. She's my wife. She's got a heart that loves the Lord, and I intend to be by her side forever.

I made a vow.